AN "OLIVER OPTIC" CHECKLIST

AN "OLIVER OPTIC" CHECKLIST

An Annotated Catalog-Index
to the Series, Nonseries Stories,
and Magazine Publications
of William Taylor Adams

Compiled by
Dolores Blythe Jones

Bibliographies and Indexes in American Literature, Number 4

Greenwood Press
Westport, Connecticut • London, England

Library of Congress Cataloging in Publication Data

Jones, Dolores Blythe.
    An "Oliver Optic" checklist.

    (Bibliographies and indexes in American literature,
ISSN 0742-6860 ; no. 4)
    Includes index.
        1. Optic, Oliver, 1822-1897—Bibliography.
    2. Children's literature, American—Bibliography.
    3. Bibliography—Children's books issued in series.
    I. Optic, Oliver, 1822-1897.   II. Title.   III. Series.
    Z8645.3.J66   1985   016.813'3   85-745
    [PS1006.A5)
    ISBN 0-313-24415-4 (lib. bdg.)

Library of Congress Catalog Card Number: 85-745
ISBN: 0-313-24415-4
ISSN: 0742-6860

First published in 1985

Greenwood Press
A division of Congressional Information Service, Inc.
88 Post Road West
Westport, Connecticut 06881

Printed in the United States of America

The paper used in this book complies with the
Permanent Paper Standard issued by the National
Information Standards Organization (Z39.48-1984).

10 9 8 7 6 5 4 3 2 1

For my parents

CONTENTS

PREFACE

An "Oliver Optic" Checklist provides a detailed listing of
titles authored by William Taylor Adams under his own name,
as well as under the pseudonyms of Oliver Optic, Gayle
Winterton, Warren T. Ashton, and Brooks McCormick. The work
includes book titles, book-length serializations, and children's magazines edited by Adams, but excludes articles,
short stories, and poetry that appeared in magazines and
newspapers (many of which were credited to additional pseudonyms attributed to Adams, such as Old Stager, Clingham Hunter,
M.D., and Irving Brown). Because this work does not set out
to determine first editions, bibliographical distinctions,
distinguishing one edition from another, have not been included. Future researchers will have to determine those facts.
   The main section of the book, CHRONOLOGICAL LIST, catalogs
Adams's titles by copyright date from 1852 to 1912. Where a
serialization was published prior to the copyright, the serialization date is used. Each title receives an entry number from
001 to 189. Depending upon the particular title, an entry
includes: the complete title, original series name, date of
publication, original publisher, story description, review
excerpts, illustrators or engravers, reprint publishers and
their series, variant titles, and holdings. Citations to
secondary sources are listed under "References." Using the
National Union Catalog (NUC) symbols, the "Locations" section
records the libraries holding any edition or reprint of Adams's
work. This chronological list also includes the children's
magazines that Adams edited, appearing under the year Adams
began to work on them. Entries in the following four sections
are cross-referenced to this section.
   The next section, AUTHOR SERIES, enumerates the series
Adams published with Lee & Shepard. Alphabetically arranged
by series name, entries include the full title, description,
and reviews for each series. In this section and the next,
each series receives its own entry with subentries for the
individual titles. The PUBLISHER SERIES lists the series
titles created by various reprint publishers. For each series,
the following information is included: the full title, the publisher, and some description of the series. The PUBLISHERS
section chronicles all publishers issuing any of William

Taylor Adams's titles, whether originally or in reprint. The
final section, SERIALIZATIONS, lists works that appeared serially in magazines or newspapers. Titles are alphabetically
grouped under the magazine or newspaper in which they appeared.

For additional information, the work concludes with four
specialized appendixes and two indexes. Appendix A, SPECIAL
COLLECTIONS DIRECTORY, lists the libraries and special collections throughout the United States that have substantial
holdings of William Taylor Adams's works. The CHRONOLOGY OF
WILLIAM TAYLOR ADAMS AND HIS PUBLISHERS, chronicles important
dates in the development of Adams's literary career and the
evolution of the Lee & Shepard firm. Appendix C, NONSERIES
BOOKS, includes those titles that, when originally published,
were not issued as part of a series. The SECONDARY BIBLI-
OGRAPHY lists articles, books, and dissertations that contain
biographical information on Adams, as well as commentary and
criticism of his works. These sources also include information
on Lee & Shepard, boys' series, and basic reference works used
in the preparation of this book.

Arranged alphabetically by artist, the first index, ILLUS-
TRATORS AND ENGRAVERS, lists the titles in which each artist
had creative input. The second, MAGAZINES, SERIES, AND SHORT-
TITLES, records all titles and title variations for Adams's
books, series, magazines, and serializations, and provides
cross-references to pertinent entry numbers throughout the
work.

This compilation offers a starting point for researchers
interested in the literary achievements of William Taylor
Adams, boys' series books, nineteenth century series fiction,
and early American children's magazines. Students and
specialists of children's literature, American literature,
popular culture, and American studies, as well as librarians,
teachers, book collectors, and booksellers will find this
book very helpful.

ACKNOWLEDGMENTS

In order to complete a project of this size, many people
have provided information and guidance. Without their help,
this compilation of William Taylor Adams's numerous works
could not have become a reality.

First and foremost, I would like to thank John M. Kelly,
Curator of the de Grummond Collection of Children's Literature. This project was started because of his observation
that William Taylor Adams had been neglected in children's
literature research. During the several years in which I
gathered information on Adams, John was always on the outlook
for new and useful reference sources. For his assistance I
am very grateful.

Marilyn Brownstein, editor at Greenwood Press, has been
extremely helpful from the initial proposal to publication;
her experienced guidance has always been appreciated. Though
unaware of her helpfulness, Deidre Johnson and her book,
Stratemeyer Pseudonyms and Series Books, have been a constant
guide in structuring the format and layout of this book.

I would also like to thank Margaret Coughlan of the Children's Literature Center, Clark Kent of Rare Books, and the
staff of the Copyright Department, all of whom provided expert
assistance during my research efforts at the Library of Congress. I am also indebted to the librarians of the Humanities
and Social Sciences divisions at the Dallas Public Library,
who gave freely of their time and expertise.

I am particularly grateful to the following people who
provided information pertaining to the holdings of their
collections: Mildred K. Abraham, University of Virginia
Library; Ruth Baldwin, Baldwin Library, University of Florida
Library; Victor A. Berch, Brandeis University Library;
Sheppard Black, Ohio University Library; Stanley W. Brown,
Dartmouth College Library; Paul Eugen Camp, University of
South Florida Library; Margaret N. Coughlan, Children's
Literature Center, Library of Congress; Ken Craven, Humanities
Research Center, The University of Texas at Austin; Jannette
Fiore, Michigan State University Library; Julanne M. Good, St.
Louis Public Library; Kathleen Horning, Cooperative Children's
Book Center, Madison, Wisconsin; Karen Nelson Hoyle, Kerlan
Collection, University of Minnesota Library; Paul T. Hudson,

The Public Library of Cincinnati and Hamilton County; Maureen
B. Lambert, Elizabeth Nesbitt Room, University of Pittsburgh;
Thomas V. Lange, The Huntington Library; Nancy Lee, Popular
Culture Collection, Bowling Green State University; Marcus A.
McCorison, American Antiquarian Society; John J. McCormick,
New Hampshire State Library; Alexandra Mason, Kenneth Spencer
Research Library, University of Kansas Libraries; Elizabeth
Patterson, Emory University; Thomas Tomczak, Milwaukee Public
Library; Debra K. Watt, Northern Illinois University Library;
and Ellen M. Whitney, Free Library of Philadelphia. I would
also like to thank the staffs at The Beinecke Rare Book and
Manuscript Library, Yale University; and the General Research
Division, New York Public Library.

I would especially like to thank my husband and son for
their support during the time I spent completing this book.

INTRODUCTION

William Taylor Adams was born in Medway, Massachusetts, on
July 30, 1822.[1] Descended from the lineage of Governor Samuel
Adams and Presidents John Adams and John Quincy Adams, William
was the son of Captain Laban and Catherine (nee Johnson) Adams.
The proprieter of Lamb Tavern in Boston, Laban Adams later
managed the Adams House. William was educated in the public
and private schools of Boston and the vicinity.

In 1841, Adams's first article was published in The Social
Monitor. This article was followed by the 1845 publication of
two temperance tales in the Washingtonian. A poem written in
1851 for the Boston Young Men's Total Abstinence Society was
published in The Flag of Our Union under the title, "1951. A
Poem. Delivered before the Mutual Admiration Society, by Oliver
Optic, M.D." This was Adams's first use of the pseudonym.

Biographical sources credit Adams with many pseudonyms.
Oliver Optic, Brooks McCormick, Warren T. Ashton, and Gayle
Winterton in particular are treated in this book. Others
including Old Stager, Irving Brown, and Clingham Hunter, which
were used for short magazine articles, travel and love stories,
are excluded here because they exceed the scope of this book.

The beginning of Adams's twenty-year association with the
Boston school system paralleled his early years of literary
development. From 1842 to 1845, Adams was a schoolmaster in
Dorchester, Massachusetts. After a short-lived stint in the
family business, he resumed his teaching career at the Boylston
School, where he became headmaster in 1860. A short time later,
he transferred to the newly established Bowditch School as
headmaster, a position he retained until 1865. In 1846, Adams
married Sarah Jenkins of Dorchester, by whom he had two
daughters.

During the 1850s, Adams continued to pursue his literary
efforts. In 1853, under the pseudonym of Warren T. Ashton,
Adams received the copyright for Hatchie, the Guardian Slave.
Hatchie was his first full-length book, which, like his next
publication, In Doors and Out, was directed toward the adult
reading audience.

Adams was becoming increasingly popular as an author. A
suggestion to write a book for boys produced The Boat Club in
1855; an immediate success, this work was eventually issued

in more than sixty different editions and remained one of the
most famous Optic titles. Five other stories written from
1856 through 1860 rounded out the BOAT CLUB SERIES. Many
other series written by William Taylor Adams and published by
Lee & Shepard were quick to follow, including THE RIVERDALE
STORIES, WOODVILLE STORIES, and THE ARMY AND NAVY STORIES.

In 1858, Adams assumed the editorship of The Student and
Schoolmate. Also the leading writer for the magazine, Adams
had a serialized story appear in each issue. Horatio Alger,
Jr., a close friend of Adams, submitted a juvenile story
concerning the Civil War entitled "Frank's Campaigns" for
publication in The Student and Schoolmate. Although Adams
turned down "Frank's Campaigns," he did ask Alger to write
short stories and poems for the magazine.[2]

By 1865, Adams found it difficult to juggle his duties as
principal of the Bowditch School and editor of The Student
and Schoolmate and still have time for his writing. In July,
he resigned from his position as principal and soon departed
on the first of twenty trips to Europe. The information and
insight gained through his first trip is displayed in YOUNG
AMERICA ABROAD, a two-series set of twelve volumes published
from 1866 through 1877.

After several Alger serializations proved very popular
with the readers, Adams relinquished his position as lead
writer of The Student and Schoolmate in 1866. Together, Adams
and Alger conceived the idea for the story which would make
Horatio Alger a household word and establish The Student and
Schoolmate as a ranking children's magazine: The January 1867
issue opened with the first installment of "Ragged Dick: or,
Street Life in New York."[3]

In 1867, Adams embarked on one of his most ambitious pro-
jects, a weekly magazine for boys and girls. Oliver Optic's
Magazine: Our Boys and Girls, edited by Oliver Optic and published weekly by Lee & Shepard, was to contain a serialized
story by the editor, as well as puzzles, articles, stories,
poetry, and anecdotes. Each "elegantly illustrated" issue
would cost five cents and a yearly subscription, $2.25. In
addition to the serials by Optic, the children were treated
to stories by Sophie May, Edward A. Samuels, Ike Parkington,
and George M. Baker. Poetry was contributed by Julia Ward
Howe. Oliver Optic's Magazine was extremely successful, and
circulation remained high, even after it became necessary to
switch to a once-a-month format in 1871. The magazine continued with increasing readership until 1875, when Lee &
Shepard experienced financial difficulties and discontinued
its publication.

In a review of Seek and Find appearing in the Nation in
1867, Adams was criticized for being a "sensational" writer.[4]
This was the first of many such attacks on his literary
style. Adams was understandably upset by this criticism and
"began the long series of editorials in which he defended
himself and his writing" using the editorial pages of Oliver
Optic's Magazine.[5]

It was not until 1875, in a famous dispute with Louisa May
Alcott, that Adams's rebuttals reached their peak. Alcott's
"Eight Cousins" was serialized in St. Nicholas during 1875.[6]

In the August installment, Alcott covertly attacked sensational stories in general and Oliver Optic specifically. Mrs.
Jessie, the mother in "Eight Cousins," disapproves of the
books that her sons have chosen to read. She tells them that
she has read at least a dozen such stories and, as a result,
feels "the writers of these popular stories intend to do good,
I have no doubt, but it seems to me they fail because their
motto is 'Be smart, and you will be rich,' instead of 'Be
honest, and you will be happy.'"[7] In response to her son
Geordie's contention that "some of them are about first-rate
boys . . . [that] go to sea and study, and sail around the
world," Mrs. Jessie says, "I have read about them, Geordie,
and though they are better than the others, I am not satisfied
with these optical delusions, as I call them."[8]
   Professional critics, whose opinions appeared in Appleton's
Journal and Scribner's Monthly, felt her attack was unwarrant-
ed.[9] Adams's own lengthy reply appeared in the September
1875 issue of Oliver Optic's Magazine. He began: "Miss Louise
[sic] M. Alcott is publishing a story in a magazine. It is
called "Eight Cousins." The title was doubtless suggested by
Miss Douglas's highly successful story "Seven Daughters," published in our magazine."[10] Adams goes on to defend himself,
using quotations and examples to illustrate that most of the
evils mentioned by Miss Alcott in "Eight Cousins" were not
found in his books, or at the very least, were greatly exag-
gerated. He then cited passages from Miss Alcott's own story
demonstrating that "Eight Cousins" displayed a fair amount of
slang and improbability. Adams ended the dispute with this
final thrust: "we must ask you to adopt the motto you recommend for others- 'Be honest and you will be happy,' instead
of the one you seem to have chosen: 'Be smart and you will be
rich.'"[11]
   Shortly afterwards, Adams had to endure the wrath of
librarians and their associates at the First Annual Conference
of the American Library Association in 1876 in Philadelphia.
The battle continued with increased fervor at the 1879 ALA
Conference, held in Boston. Adams, as well as other "sensational" writers of the period, became the focus of this
controversy concerning the desirability and value of fiction
in the public libraries of the United States.
   Samuel Swett Green[12] spoke out as a proponent of both
fiction and Oliver Optic in his address: "I have no doubt that
harm comes to some young men from reading the books of Oliver
Optic, and I know that a good deal of time is wasted in reading them . . . . But I take it comparatively few persons are
deceived by these books, while the great bulk of readers get
them from merely the enjoyment of the story."[13]
   Others who addressed the 1879 Conference in favor of Optic
and fiction were T. W. Higginson, James Freeman Clarke, and
Charles A. Cutter. The opponents of Optic and the literary
style he represented were Kate Gannett Wells, Charles Francis
Adams, Jr., and William P. Atkinson. Atkinson could not agree
with Higginson's "'rather rose colored view of the influence
of the Oliver Optics of this day.' He did not believe the
really clever boys were much addicted to Oliver Opticism,
and thought it had a mischievious influence on the limp mind

of the ordinary boy. 'He settled down into it and does not rise above it: it is well if he does not sink below it.'"[14]

By the early 1880s, Adams's books were not allowed on the shelves of many public libraries, although the same books were receiving quite acceptable reviews in leading literary magazines and maintaining high sales figures.

Throughout his literary career, Adams received considerable criticism from teachers, librarians, and literary critics, who questioned his characterizations, as well as the probability of his plots. The morality of his characters was beyond question, always living up to Adams's writing motto, "First God, then country, then friends." Of his writing Adams once said:

> I have a fixed standard before me in writing all my books, from which I have never deviated. My aim has been to construct a tale interesting and exciting enough to catch and hold the attention of young people, and yet never to entrap them into sympathy with evil-doers or to encourage in them admiration for bold and lawless acts. I have never made a hero whose moral character or whose lack of high aims could mislead the young reader.[15]

Despite the varied criticisms, Adams continued to please his young public with series such as the GREAT WESTERN SERIES, BOAT-BUILDER SERIES, ALL-OVER-THE-WORLD LIBRARY, THE BLUE AND THE GRAY, and THE BLUE AND THE GRAY ON LAND. The twelve volumes of the two BLUE AND GRAY SERIES met with outstanding reviews. The critics of the late 1880s were the young boys of the 1860s, who had voraciously read every Oliver Optic they could find. At the time of his death, Adams had completed five of the six volumes for THE BLUE AND THE GRAY ON LAND SERIES. An Undivided Union was completed by a new and relatively unknown Lee & Shepard author, Edward Stratemeyer.

Raymond L. Kilgour, in Lee & Shepard: Publishers for the People, credits Adams with creating the mass production method in children's books.[16] Lee & Shepard have been cited for establishing the series as a successful mode of young adult publishing, much to the dismay of librarians and teachers.

Adams was certainly a mainstay in the financial success of Lee & Shepard; his books remained a large portion of their list until the early 1900s. The 123 novels by Adams that appeared in Lee & Shepard's catalog were transferred in 1904 to the new firm of Lothrop, Lee & Shepard. They continued publication of 19 original series created by Oliver Optic. At the time of his death in 1897, it was estimated that two million copies of his books had been sold, more than that of any other author living at the time.[17] Lee & Shepard records show that Adams's titles sold more than 100,000 copies per year at the height of their popularity.

As the Boston Budget said of Adams's influence, "In the literary life of America he has been an unique figure, establishing his greatness in the hearts of the boys and the girls, and laying a stone of immortality that shall stand as long as the present generation may exist."[18]

Although Oliver Optic may be unknown to the more sophisticated young readers of today, his impact and influence on the youth of yesterday should be remembered.

Notes

1. Raymond L. Kilgour, Lee & Shepard: Publishers for the People ([s.l.]: Shoe String Press, 1965), p. 289. Biographical sources differ on the place of Adams's birth. Both Medway or Bellingham are often mentioned. Kilgour says they are one in the same.
2. Edwin P. Hoyt, Horatio's Boys: The Life and Works of Horatio Alger, Jr. (Radnor, Pennsylvania: Chilton Book Co., 1974), p. 40.
3. Ibid., pp. 73-74.
4. [Review of Seek and Find]. Nation, December 26, 1867, p. 524.
5. Richard L. Darling, The Rise of Children's Book Reviewing in America, 1855-1881 (New York: R. R. Bowker, 1968), p. 33.
6. Louisa May Alcott, "Eight cousins," St. Nicholas, January-October, 1875.
7. Alcott, "Eight cousins," St. Nicholas, August 1875, p. 616-17.
8. Ibid.
9. Darling, The Rise of Children's Book Reviewing in America, p. 37.
10. William T. Adams, "Sensational books," Oliver Optic's Magazine, September 1875, p. 718.
11. Ibid.
12. Samuel Swett Green, 1837-1918, librarian of the Worcester Free Public Library, was one of the originators (and president, 1891) of the American Library Association.
13. Samuel Swett Green, "Sensational fiction in public libraries," Library Journal, September-October 1879, p. 349.
14. Esther Jane Carrier, Fiction in Public Libraries, 1876-1900 (New York: Scarecrow Press, 1965), p. 198.
15. Kilgour, Lee & Shepard, p. 240.
16. Ibid., p. 270.
17. "Oliver Optic passes away," New York Herald, March 28, 1897, section 3, p. 4.
18. "The author of one hundred successful books," The Literary Digest, April 10, 1897, p. 700.

LIST OF ABBREVIATIONS

AS	Author Series	L&S	Lee & Shepard
b.	born	LC	Library of Congress
c	copyright	NUC	National Union Catalog
ca.	circa	P	Publisher
d.	died	PS	Publisher Series
fl.	flourished	S	Serializations

NATIONAL UNION CATALOG (NUC) SYMBOLS

CSmH	The Huntington Library
CtY	Yale University, Beinecke Rare Books
DLC	Library of Congress
FTS	University of South Florida Library
FU	University of Florida, Baldwin Library
GEU	Emory University Library
IDekN	Northern Illinois University Library
KU	University of Kansas Library, Spencer Library
MB	Boston Public Library
MWA	American Antiquarian Society
MWalB	Brandeis University Library
MiEM	Michigan State University Library
MnU	University of Minnesota, Children's Literature Research Collection
MoS	St. Louis Public Library
MsHAu	University of Southern Mississippi, de Grummond Collection
NHD	Dartmouth College Library
NN	New York Public Library
Nh	New Hampshire State Library
OAU	Ohio University Library
OBgU	Bowling Green State University, Popular Culture Collection
OC	Public Library of Cincinnati and Hamilton County
PP	Free Library of Philadelphia
PPiU	University of Pittsburgh Library, Nesbitt Room
TxU	University of Texas at Austin, Humanities Research Center
ViU	University of Virginia Library
WM	Milwaukee Public Library
WU	Cooperative Children's Book Center

AN ''OLIVER OPTIC''
CHECKLIST

CHRONOLOGICAL LIST

1852

001. Hatchie, the guardian slave: or, The heiress of
      Bellevue. A tale of the Mississippi and the South-
      west by Warren T. Ashton. B.B. Mussey and Co. and
      R.B. Fitts and Co., c1852.

   Copyright dated November 23, 1852, granted in the District
   of Massachusetts to R.B. Fitts. Copy deposited April 2,
   1853. Preface dated November 18, 1852.

Description: "...The tale was written before the appearance
   of 'Uncle Tom's Cabin,' - before negro literature had become a mania in the community. It was not designed to
   illustrate the evils or the blessings of slavery. It is,
   as its title page imports, a tale;...But, as its locale
   is the South, and its principal character a slave, the
   story incidentally portrays some features of slavery..."
   [preface].

Illustrations: 3 plates; 1 signed "Fox."

   Adams's first book for adults, for which he earned
   $37.50.

Other Printings: Books for Libraries Press (THE BLACK
   HERITAGE LIBRARY COLLECTION) / Research Publications
   (WRIGHT AMERICAN FICTION v.2 [1851-1875] reel A-4 no.25).

References: Wright II, #25.

Locations: CSmH, CtY, DLC, GEU, MB, MWA, MsHAu, NHD, ViU

1854

002. In doors and out: or, Views from the chimney corner.
      Brown, Bazin and Co., c1854.

Copyright dated September 4, 1854, granted in the District
of Massachusetts to Brown, Bazin and Co. Copy deposited
December 29, 1854. Copyright renewal #13315 dated December 16, 1875, granted to Lee & Shepard for a new edition.
Two copies deposited December 27, 1875. Preface (new ed.)
dated October 26, 1875.

Contents: Getting an indorser -- Good for nothings -- Two
daguerreotypes -- Six hundred a year -- The new minister
-- Out nights -- Bring flowers -- The domestic element --
Bang up -- The new cloak -- Everything comfortable --
Family jars -- Life insurance -- Last day of grace --
Montague and lady -- Taking the newspapers -- Cigars for
two -- Out of business -- Six months after date -- World
of trouble -- Send for the doctor -- Four kinds of cake --
Extremes meet -- The mercantile angel -- Confessions of a
conceited man -- The bachelor beau -- The grand reception
ball -- Marrying a beggar.

Reprinted in part from various periodicals.

Illustrations: Anonymous.

Reviews: "Differing from other books of this popular author
   in that it is intended for adult readers, while the others
   are written for young people. It contains about thirty
   interesting stories of a domestic order...We recommend the
   book heartily..." Vermont Record. [per L&S ad].

"As a writer of domestic stories,... Adams made his mark
even before he became so immensely popular through his
splendid books for the young...They are written in a
spirited style, impart valuable practical lessons, and are
of the most lively interest..." Boston Home Journal.
[per L&S ad].

"Excellent stories, all of which might have been drawn
from actual life, are to be found in this volume. Like
all of Oliver Optic's books, it may be safely placed in
the hands of young people. Some of the sketches, such as
'Good-for-nothings,' might be read with as much profit as
amusement by grown-up persons, especially those who are
continually complaining about servant-girls." Catholic
World 22 (April 1876): 720.

"With these two volumes [In-Doors and out and Living too
fast] the publisher will commence the issue of 'The
Household Library' intending to embrace a series of
attractive and wholesome romances, for the family circle."
Publisher's Weekly Book Fair Supplement, 1876.

   Also reviewed in New England Journal of Education 3
   (1 January 1876): 12.

Some of these same titles appear in Getting an indorser
(95) and Marrying a beggar (11).

Other Printings: Higgins and Bradley / Higgins, Bradley and
    Dayton / Lee & Shepard (THE HOUSEHOLD LIBRARY v.1) /
    Lothrop, Lee & Shepard / Research Publications (WRIGHT
    AMERICAN FICTION v.2 [1851-1875] reel A-4 no.26).

References: Wright II, #26.

Locations: CSmH, CtY, DLC, FTS, FU, MB, MWA, MnU, NHD, NN,
    OAU, TxU, ViU

003. The boat club: or, The bunkers of Rippleton. A tale for
      boys. Brown, Bazin and Co., c1854. BOAT CLUB SERIES
      v.1.

    Copyright dated October 5, 1854, granted in the District
    of Massachusetts to William T. Adams. Copy deposited
    December 29, 1854. Copyright #10285 dated June 21, 1882,
    for renewal on October 5, 1882. Copyright #61146 dated
    1896. Copyright #A20166 dated August 13, 1900. Two
    copies deposited at LC on August 18, 1900. Preface dated
    September 20, 1854.

Description: "...[the author] has endeavoured to combine
    healthy moral lessons with a sufficient amount of exciting
    interest to render the story attractive to the young..."
    [preface].

Illustrations: Early printings are signed by John Andrew,
    probably as engraver; later printings are signed [John]
    Andrew-[John] Filmer. In 1862, Lee & Shepard advertised
    that their reprint was illustrated by Hammatt Billings.
    A McLoughlin Brothers reprint was illustrated by Enos B.
    Comstock.

Other Printings: American News (EMPIRE EDITION) / Brown,
    Taggard and Chase / Burt / Caldwell (BEST BOOKS FOR BOYS
    #8; BOAT CLUB SERIES; FAMOUS BOOKS FOR BOYS #1) / Carlton
    Press (GENEVA BOOK) / Cassell, Petter and Galpin / Conkey
    / Crosby, Nichols, Lee / Donohue (BOUND TO WIN SERIES;
    FIRESIDE HENTY SERIES; OLIVER OPTIC SERIES #3) / Donohue,
    Henneberry / Federal (BOYS' POPULAR LIBRARY; "LUPTON" GILT
    TOP SERIES) / Gedalge Jeune (SCENES DE LA VIE AMERICAINE)
    / Henneberry (BOAT CLUB SERIES) / Homewood / Hurst (OLIVER
    OPTIC BOOKS) / International / Lee & Shepard (AMERICAN
    BOYS' SERIES #5) / Lee & Shepard; Charles T. Dillingham
    (BOAT CLUB SERIES) / Lee & Shepard; Lee, Shepard & Dill-
    ingham (BOAT CLUB SERIES) / Lothrop, Lee & Shepard
    (AMERICAN BOYS' SERIES #5; BOAT CLUB SERIES; OLIVER OPTIC
    SERIES #7) / Lupton (GOLD SERIES) / McKay (BOYS' POPULAR
    LIBRARY #3) / McLoughlin (OLIVER OPTIC'S BOAT CLUB SERIES)
    / Mershon (BOAT CLUB SERIES) / George Munro's Sons (LUCKY
    SERIES) / New York Book Co. (OLIVER OPTIC BOOKS) / New
    York Publishing Co. / Ogilvie / Phillips, Sampson / Rickey,
    Mallory; Crosby, Nichols, Lee; Phinney, Blakeman & Mason
    (LIBRARY FOR YOUNG PEOPLE) / Street & Smith (ALGER SERIES

#159; BOYS' POPULAR LIBRARY #3; MEDAL LIBRARY #1).

Note: This title was first published by Brown, Bazin and Co.
   until their collapse in 1857. Publication was then taken
   over by Phillips, Sampson & Co. in 1859 just as they were
   to go out of business. William Lee reprinted the title
   in the Fall of 1860 under the imprint of Crosby, Nichols,
   Lee & Co. The book was dropped when Lee left the firm
   in 1861. The plates were purchased by Lee & Shepard and
   reprinted in 1862.

Variant Titles: The boat club: or, Good·fellows all. (ALGER
   SERIES); Le club des canotiers: ou, Les bunkers de
   Rippleton. (French translation published by Gedalge).

Locations: CtY, DLC, FTS, FU, GEU, IDekN, KU, MB, MWA, MiEM,
   MnU, MoS, MsHAu, MWalB, NHD, NN, Nh, OAU, OBgU, OC, PP,
   PPiU, TxU, ViU, WM

                          1856

004.   All aboard: or, Life on the lake. A sequel to "The boat
       club."   Brown, Bazin and Co., c1856. BOAT CLUB
       SERIES v.2.

   Copyright dated January 2, 1856, granted in the District
   of Massachusetts to William T. Adams. Copy deposited January 2, 1856. Copyright renewal #A12041 dated January 2,
   1884. Copyright #A20147 dated 1900. Preface dated 1855.

Description: "'All Aboard' was written to gratify the reason-
   able curiosity of the readers of the 'Boat Club,' to know
   what occurred at Woodlake during the second season; and
   though it is a sequel, it has no direct connection with
   its predecessor. The Introduction in the first chapter
   contains a brief synopsis of the principal events of the
   first season..." [L&S ad].

Illustrations: Early printings are signed John Andrew,
   probably as engraver; later printings are signed [John]
   Andrew-[John] Filmer. In 1862, Lee & Shepard advertised
   that their reprint was illustrated by Hammatt Billings.
   A McLoughlin Brothers reprint was illustrated by Enos B.
   Comstock.

Other Printings: American News (EMPIRE EDITION) / Burt /
   Caldwell (BEST BOOKS FOR BOYS #4; BOAT CLUB SERIES; FAMOUS
   BOOKS FOR BOYS #1) / Conkey / Crosby, Nichols, Lee /
   Donohue (BOUND TO WIN SERIES; OLIVER OPTIC SERIES #1) /
   Federal (BOYS' POPULAR LIBRARY; "LUPTON" GILT TOP SERIES)
   / Henneberry (BOAT CLUB SERIES) / Homewood / Hurst (OLIVER
   OPTIC BOOKS) / International / Lee & Shepard (AMERICAN
   BOYS' SERIES #2) / Lee & Shepard; Charles T. Dillingham
   (BOAT CLUB SERIES) / Lee, Shepard & Dill-
   ingham (BOAT CLUB SERIES) / Lothrop, Lee & Shepard

(AMERICAN BOYS' SERIES #2; BOAT CLUB SERIES; OLIVER OPTIC
SERIES #8) / Lupton (GOLD SERIES) / McKay (BOYS' POPULAR
LIBRARY #1) / McLoughlin (OLIVER OPTIC'S BOAT CLUB SERIES)
/ Mershon (BOAT CLUB SERIES) / New York Book Co. (OLIVER
OPTIC BOOKS) / Ogilvie / Phillips, Sampson / Rickey,
Mallory; Crosby, Nichols, Lee; Phinney, Blakeman & Mason
(LIBRARY FOR YOUNG PEOPLE) / Street & Smith (ALGER SERIES
#160; BOYS' POPULAR LIBRARY #1; MEDAL LIBRARY #3).

Note: This title was first published by Brown, Bazin and Co.
    until their collapse in 1857. Publication was then taken
    over by Phillips, Sampson & Co. in 1859 just as they were
    to go out of business. William Lee reprinted the title
    in the Fall of 1860 under the imprint of Crosby, Nichols,
    Lee & Co. The book was dropped when Lee left the firm in
    1861. The plates were purchased by Lee & Shepard and
    reprinted in 1862.

Variant Titles: All aboard: or, A cruise for fun. (ALGER
    SERIES).

Locations: CtY, DLC, FTS, FU, GEU, IDekN, KU, MB, MWA, MiEM,
    MnU, MoS, MsHAu, MWalB, NHD, NN, Nh, OAU, OBgU, OC, PP,
    TxU, ViU, WM

005. Now or never: or, The adventures of Bobby Bright. A
      story for young folks. Brown, Bazin and Co., c1856.
      BOAT CLUB SERIES v.3.

    Copyright dated December 11, 1856, granted in the District
    of Massachusetts to William T. Adams. Copy deposited
    December 11, 1856. Copyright #20333 dated October 9, 1884
    for renewal on December 11, 1884. Copyright #A20156 dated
    1900. Preface dated November 15, 1856.

Description: "The story contained in this volume is a record
    of youthful struggles, not only in the world without, but
    in the world within; and the success of the little hero
    is not merely a gathering up of wealth and honors, but a
    triumph over the temptations that beset the pilgrim on the
    plain of life. The attainment of worldly prosperity is not
    the truest victory; and the author has endeavored to make
    the interest of his story depend more on the hero's devo-
    tion to principles than on his success in business."
    [preface].

Illustrations: Early printings are signed by John Andrew,
    probably as engraver; later printings are signed [John]
    Andrew-[John] Filmer. In 1862, Lee & Shepard advertised
    that their reprint was illustrated by Hammatt Billings.

Other Printings: American News (EMPIRE EDITION) / Burt /
    Caldwell (BEST BOOKS FOR BOYS #36, BOAT CLUB SERIES) /
    Conkey / Crosby, Nichols, Lee / Donohue (BOUND TO WIN
    SERIES; BOYS BANNER SERIES #11; OLIVER OPTIC SERIES #9) /

Federal (BOYS' POPULAR LIBRARY; "LUPTON" GILT TOP SERIES)
/ Henneberry (BOAT CLUB SERIES) / Homewood / Hurst (OLIVER
OPTIC BOOKS) / International / Lee & Shepard (AMERICAN
BOYS' SERIES #31) / Lee & Shepard; Charles T. Dillingham
(BOAT CLUB SERIES) / Lee & Shepard; Lee, Shepard &
Dillingham (BOAT CLUB SERIES) / Lothrop, Lee & Shepard
(AMERICAN BOYS' SERIES #31; BOAT CLUB SERIES; OLIVER OPTIC
SERIES #9) / McKay (BOYS' POPULAR LIBRARY #31) / McLough-
lin (OLIVER OPTIC'S BOAT CLUB SERIES) / Mershon (BOAT CLUB
SERIES) / New York Book Co. (OLIVER OPTIC BOOKS) / New
York Publishing Co. / Ogilvie / Phillips, Sampson / Rickey,
Mallory; Crosby, Nichols, Lee; Phinney, Blakeman & Mason
(LIBRARY FOR YOUNG PEOPLE) / Street & Smith (ALGER SERIES
#161; BOYS' POPULAR LIBRARY #31; MEDAL LIBRARY #5).

Note: This title was first published by Brown, Bazin and Co.
until their collapse in 1857. Publication was then taken
over by Phillips, Sampson & Co. in 1859 just as they were
to go out of business. William Lee reprinted the title in
the Fall of 1860 under the imprint of Crosby, Nichols, Lee
& Co. The book was dropped when Lee left the firm in 1861.
The plates were purchased by Lee & Shepard and reprinted
in 1862.

Variant Titles: Now or never: or, The reward of friendship.
(ALGER SERIES).

Locations: CSmH, CtY, DLC, FTS, FU, GEU, IDekN, KU, MB, MWA,
MiEM, MnU, MoS, MsHAu, NHD, NN, Nh, OAU, OBgU, OC, PP,
PPiU, ViU, WM

1857

006. Try again: or, The trials and triumphs of Harry West. A
story for young folks. Brown, Taggard and Chase,
c1857. BOAT CLUB SERIES v.4.

Copyright dated April 3, 1857, granted in the District of
Massachusetts to William T. Adams. No record of deposit.
Copyright renewal #15797 dated July 23, 1885. Two copies
deposited at LC on July 28, 1887. Preface dated March 26,
1857.

Description: "The story of Harry West is a record of youthful
experience designed to illustrate the necessity and the
results of perseverance in well doing. The true success
of life is the attainment of a pure and exalted character;
and he who at three-score-and-ten has won nothing but
wealth and a name, has failed to achieve the noblest
purpose of his being. This is the moral of the story
contained in this volume." [L&S ad].

Illustrations: Early printings signed John Andrew, probably
as engraver; later printings signed [John] Andrew-[John]
Filmer. In 1862, Lee & Shepard advertised that their re-

print was illustrated by Hammatt Billings. A McLoughlin Brothers reprint was illustrated by W.E. Burford.

Other Printings: American News (EMPIRE EDITION) / Burt / Caldwell (BOAT CLUB SERIES) / Conkey / Crosby, Nichols, Lee / Donohue (BOUND TO WIN SERIES; BOY'S LIBERTY SERIES #18; OLIVER OPTIC SERIES #16) / Federal (BOYS' POPULAR LIBRARY; "LUPTON" GILT TOP SERIES) / Gedalge (TABLEAUX DE LA VIE AMERICAINE) / Henneberry (BOAT CLUB SERIES) / Homewood / Hurst (OLIVER OPTIC BOOKS) / Lee & Shepard (AMERICAN BOYS' SERIES #40) / Lee & Shepard; Charles T. Dillingham (BOAT CLUB SERIES) / Lee & Shepard; Lee, Shepard & Dillingham (BOAT CLUB SERIES) / Lothrop, Lee & Shepard (AMERICAN BOYS' SERIES #40; BOAT CLUB SERIES; OLIVER OPTIC SERIES #10) / McKay (BOYS' POPULAR LIBRARY #45) / McLoughlin / Mershon (BOAT CLUB SERIES) / New York Book Co. (OLIVER OPTIC BOOKS) / Perkins / Phillips, Sampson / Rickey, Mallory; Crosby, Nichols, Lee; Phinney, Blakeman & Mason (LIBRARY FOR YOUNG PEOPLE) / Street & Smith (ALGER SERIES #162; BOYS' POPULAR LIBRARY #45; MEDAL LIBRARY #9).

Note: This title was first published by Brown, Taggard and Chase. Publication was then taken over by Phillips, Sampson & Co. in 1859 just as they were to go out of business. William Lee reprinted the title in the Fall of 1860 under the imprint of Crosby, Nichols, Lee & Co. The book was dropped when Lee left the firm in 1861. The plates were purchased by Lee & Shepard and reprinted in 1862.

Variant Titles: Try again: or, The boy who did right. (ALGER SERIES); A recommencer! (French translation published by Gedalge Jeune).

Locations: CtY, DLC, FTS, FU, IDekN, KU, MB, MWA, MiEM, MnU, MoS, MsHAu, MWalB, NHD, NN, Nh, OAU, OBgU, OC, PP, TxU, ViU, WM

1858

007. The student and schoolmate; an illustrated monthly for our boys & girls.

Edited by Oliver Optic 1858-1866? [1872].
(There is a controversy concerning the year in which Adams's editorial duties ceased. The subject was never mentioned in The Student and Schoolmate; but, in Oliver Optic's Magazine (v.1,#1, January 5, 1867) Adams stated that he wrote for no other juvenile publication.)

Dates: 1855-1872.
Editors: N.A. Calkins (1855-1857); William T. Adams (1858-1866? [1872]).

Publishers: Robinson & Richardson, Boston; Calkins and Stiles,
    New York (1855-1856); James Robinson & Co., Boston (1857-
    1858); Robinson, Greene & Co., Boston (1859); Galen James
    & Co., Boston (1860-1862); Joseph H. Allen, Boston (1863-
    1872).

References: R. Gordon Kelly. Children's periodicals of the
    United States. Westport, CT: Greenwood Press, 1983.
    Betty L. Lyons. "A history of children's secular magazines
    published in the United States from 1789-1899." (Ph.D.
    dissertation, Johns Hopkins University, 1942).

Frequent Contributors: William T. Adams, Horatio Alger, Jane
    Austin, Charles Carleton Coffin, Francis Forrester, Grace
    Greenwood, Gail Hamilton, Caroline M. Hewins, Sophie May,
    John Townsend Trowbridge.

Illustration: There was very little illustration in this
    magazine.

Features: Two unique features were an original dialogue
    suitable for school presentation and an oratorical exer-
    cise, marked for inflection and emphasis; accompanied
    by a gesture chart. Serialized stories were present in
    each issue, as was Father Forrester's Chit-Chat. All of
    these features were later used by Adams in Oliver Optic's
    Magazine (54).

Other information: In addition to his editorial tasks, Adams
    was also a regular contributor to the magazine. Beginning
    in 1858, each volume featured a serialized story by Oliver
    Optic. See entries 8, 10, 12, 14, 16, 17, 31, 33, 38, 39,
    41, and 47.

Locations: CSmH, CtY, DLC, FU, KU, MB, MWA, MnU, NN, WM

008. "Things worth knowing."

    Appeared serially in The Student and Schoolmate,
    May - October 1858.

    This title has not been located in book form.

009. Poor and proud: or, The fortunes of Katy Redburn. A
      story for young folks. Phillips, Sampson & Co., c1858.
      BOAT CLUB SERIES v.5.

    Copyright dated November 22, 1858, granted in the Dis-
    trict of Massachusetts to Phillips, Sampson & Co. Copy
    deposited November 22, 1858. Preface dated September
    29, 1858.

Description: "The history of a smart girl, where fortunes
    are made to depend upon her good principles, her polite-

ness, her determined perseverance, and her overcoming
that foolish pride, which is a snare to the feet. In
these respects she is a worthy example for the young."
[L&S ad].

Illustrations: Early printings signed by [John] Andrew-
[John] Filmer, probably as engravers. In 1862, Lee &
Shepard advertised that their reprint was illustrated
by Hammatt Billings.

Other Printings: Burt / Caldwell (BOAT CLUB SERIES) / Conkey /
Crosby, Nichols, Lee / Donohue (BOUND TO WIN SERIES; BOYS
LIBERTY SERIES #12; OLIVER OPTIC SERIES #11) / Federal
("LUPTON" GILT TOP SERIES) / Henneberry (BOAT CLUB
SERIES) / Homewood / Hurst (OLIVER OPTIC BOOKS) / Lee &
Shepard (AMERICAN BOYS' SERIES #32) / Lee & Shepard;
Charles T. Dillingham (BOAT CLUB SERIES) / Lee & Shepard;
Lee, Shepard & Dillingham (BOAT CLUB SERIES) / Lothrop,
Lee & Shepard (AMERICAN BOYS' SERIES #32; BOAT CLUB SERIES;
OLIVER OPTIC SERIES #11) / Mershon (BOAT CLUB SERIES) /
New York Book Co. (OLIVER OPTIC BOOKS) / New York Publish-
ing Co. (EMPIRE EDITION) / Ogilvie / Rickey, Mallory;
Crosby, Nichols, Lee; Phinney, Blakeman & Mason (LIBRARY
FOR YOUNG PEOPLE) / Street & Smith (ALGER SERIES #163;
MEDAL LIBRARY #46) / Wanamaker (WANAMAKER'S YOUNG PEOPLE'S
LIBRARY).

Note: This title was first published by Phillips, Sampson &
Co., before they went out of business in 1859. William
Lee reprinted the title in the Fall of 1860 under the
imprint of Crosby, Nichols, Lee & Co. The book was dropped
when Lee left the firm in 1861. The plates were purchased
by Lee & Shepard and reprinted in 1862.

Locations: CSmH, DLC, FTS, FU, GEU, IDekN, MB, MWA, MiEM, MnU,
MoS, MsHAu, MWalB, NHD, NN, Nh, OAU, OBgU, OC, PP, TxU,
ViU, WM

010. "The magic lantern: or, Winter evening lessons."

Appeared serially in The Student and Schoolmate,
December 1858 - June 1859.

This title has not been located in book form.

1859

011. Marrying a beggar: or, The angel in disguise and other
tales by William T. Adams. Wentworth, Hewes & Co.,
c1859.

Originally published as In doors and out (2) with first
and last titles transposed.

Some of the same titles appeared in <u>Getting an indorser and other stories</u> (95).

Reprinted in part from various periodicals.

Contents: Marrying a beggar -- Good for nothings -- Two daguerreotypes -- Six hundred a year -- The new minister -- Out nights -- Bring flowers -- The domestic element -- Bang up -- The new cloak -- Everything comfortable -- Family jars -- Life insurance -- Last day of grace -- Montague and lady -- Taking the newspapers -- Cigars for two -- Out of business -- Six months after date -- World of trouble -- Send for the doctor -- Four kinds of cake -- Extremes meet -- The mercantile angel -- Confessions of a conceited man -- The bachelor beau -- The grand reception ball -- Getting an indorser.

Other Printings: Thayer and Eldridge.

References: Wright II, #26 (note).

Locations: CSmH, MWA, NN

012. "Frank Howard's journey in the United States."

Appeared serially in <u>The Student and Schoolmate,</u> January - April and June - July 1859.

This title has not been located in book form.

1860

013. <u>The universal speaker: containing a collection of speeches, dialogues and recitations, adapted to the use of schools, academies, and social circles</u> edited by N.A. Calkins and W.T. Adams. Brown, Taggard and Chase, c1860.

Other printings: Taggard and Thompson.

Locations: MB

014. "The young philosopher."

Appeared serially in <u>The Student and Schoolmate,</u> January - December 1860.

This title has not been located in book form.

015. <u>Little by little: or, The cruise of the Flyaway. A story for young folks.</u> Crosby, Nichols, Lee & Co., c1860. BOAT CLUB SERIES v.6.

Copyright dated October 4, 1860, granted in the District
of Massachusetts to William T. Adams. Copy deposited
November 12, 1860. Copyright #13523 dated May 8, 1888 for
renewal on October 4, 1888. Preface dated August 28, 1860.

Description: "Paul Duncan, the hero of this volume, is a
    nautical young gentleman, and most of the events of the
    story occur upon the water, and possess that exciting
    and captivating character for which this author's books
    are famous. But the author hopes that something more
    than exciting incidents will be found upon his pages;
    that though he has seldom, if ever, gone out of his way
    to define the moral quality, or measure the moral
    quantity, of the words and deeds of his characters, the
    story will not be found wanting in a true Christian
    spirit." [L&S ad].

Illustrations: Early printings signed [John] Andrew- [John]
    Filmer, probably as engravers. In 1862, Lee & Shepard
    advertised that their reprint was illustrated by Hammatt
    Billings. A McLoughlin Brothers reprint was illustrated
    by W.E. Burford.

Other Printings: Burt / Caldwell (BOAT CLUB SERIES) / Conkey /
    Crosby, Nichols, Lee / Donohue (BOUND TO WIN SERIES; BOYS
    BANNER SERIES #9; BOYS LIBERTY SERIES #8; OLIVER OPTIC
    SERIES #8) / Federal (BOYS' POPULAR LIBRARY) / Henneberry
    (BOAT CLUB SERIES) / Homewood / Hurst (ARGYLE SERIES;
    CAMBRIDGE CLASSICS; GILT TOP SERIES; LAURELHURST SERIES;
    LIBRARY FOR YOUNG PEOPLE #6; OLIVER OPTIC BOOKS; YOUNG
    AMERICA LIBRARY FOR BOYS) / Lee & Shepard (AMERICAN BOYS'
    SERIES #27) / Lee & Shepard, Charles T. Dillingham (BOAT
    CLUB SERIES) / Lee & Shepard; Lee, Shepard & Dillingham
    (BOAT CLUB SERIES) / Lothrop, Lee & Shepard (AMERICAN
    BOYS' SERIES #27; BOAT CLUB SERIES; OLIVER OPTIC SERIES
    #12) / McKay (BOYS' POPULAR LIBRARY #24) / McLoughlin /
    Mershon (BOAT CLUB SERIES) / New York Book Co. (OLIVER
    OPTIC BOOKS) / Ogilvie / Rickey, Mallory; Crosby, Nichols,
    Lee; Phinney, Blakeman & Mason (LIBRARY FOR YOUNG PEOPLE) /
    Saalfield / Street & Smith (ALGER SERIES #164; AMERICAN
    BOYS' LIBRARY; BOYS' POPULAR LIBRARY #24; MEDAL LIBRARY
    #160).

Note: This title was first published by Crosby, Nichols,
    Lee & Co. The book was dropped when Lee left the firm in
    1861. The plates were purchased by Lee & Shepard and
    reprinted in 1862.

Variant Titles: Little by little: or, When success beckons.
    (ALGER SERIES).

Locations: CtY, DLC, FTS, FU, IDekN, KU, MB, MWA, MiEM, MnU,
    MoS, MsHAu, MWalE, NHD, NN, Nh, OAU, OBgU, OC, PP, WM

1861

016.   "The young travelers."

Appeared serially in The Student and Schoolmate,
January - August 1861.   ·

This title has not been located in book form.

1862

017.   "The widow and her son: a New Year's story."

Appeared serially in The Student and Schoolmate,
January 1862 - ??.

This title has not been located in book form.

018.   The little merchant. A story for little folks. Lee &
         Shepard, c1862. RIVERDALE STORIES v.1.

Copyright dated May 12, 1862, granted in the District of
Massachusetts to William T. Adams. Copy deposited October
18, 1864.

A small book designed for very young children.

018a.   Story entitled "The Newsboy" on pp. 87-96.

Illustrations: Hammatt Billings; engraved by John Andrew.

Other Printings: Conkey / Lee & Shepard (RIVERDALE STORY
    BOOKS v.1) / Lee & Shepard; Charles T. Dillingham
    (RIVERDALE STORIES) / Lothrop, Lee & Shepard (RIVERDALE
    STORIES).

    A compilation entitled The little merchant was published
    by Hurst on September 16, 1905.
    Contents: The little merchant -- The newsboy -- The
    gold thimble -- Whip-poor-Will -- Uncle Ben -- The
    Christmas gift. (see 20, 22, 28).
    Hurst (OLIVER OPTIC BOOKS; RIVERDALE STORIES; YOUNG
    AMERICA LIBRARY FOR BOYS).

Locations: DLC, FTS, FU, KU, MB, MWA, MnU, MsHAu, NHD, NN,
    OBgU, TxU

Locations for Hurst compilation: WM

019.   The young voyagers. A story for little folks. Lee &
         Shepard, c1862. RIVERDALE STORIES v.2.

Copyright dated May 12, 1862, granted in the District of

Massachusetts to William T. Adams. Copy deposited October 18, 1864. Copyright renewal #779? dated 1890, granted to William T. Adams.

A small book designed for very young children.

Illustrations: Hammatt Billings; engraved by John Andrew.

Other Printings: Lee & Shepard (RIVERDALE STORY BOOKS v.2) / Lee & Shepard; Charles T. Dillingham (RIVERDALE STORIES) / Lothrop, Lee & Shepard (RIVERDALE STORIES).

See The do-somethings (29) for compilation issued by Hurst.

Locations: DLC, FU, MB, MWA, MnU, MoS, MsHAu, NHD, NN, OBgU, WM

020. The Christmas gift. A story for little folks. Lee & Shepard, c1862. RIVERDALE STORIES v.3.

Copyright dated May 12, 1862, granted in the District of Massachusetts to William T. Adams. Copy deposited October 18, 1864.

A small book designed for very young children.

Illustrations: Hammatt Billings; engraved by John Andrew.

Other Printings: Conkey / Lee & Shepard (FLORA LEE STORY BOOKS v.1) / Lee & Shepard; Charles T. Dillingham (RIVERDALE STORIES) / Lothrop, Lee & Shepard (RIVERDALE STORIES).

See The little merchant (18) for compilation issued by Hurst.

Locations: CtY, DLC, FU, IDekN, MB, MWA, MnU, NHD, Nh, OBgU, PP

021. Dolly and I. A story for little folks. Lee & Shepard, c1862. RIVERDALE STORIES v.4.

Copyright dated May 12, 1862, granted in the District of Massachusetts to William T. Adams. Copy deposited October 18, 1864. Copyright renewal #7796 dated 1890, granted to William T. Adams.

A small book designed for very young children.

Illustrations: Hammatt Billings; engraved by John Andrew.

Other Printings: Lee & Shepard (RIVERDALE STORY BOOKS v.3) / Lee & Shepard; Charles T. Dillingham (RIVERDALE STORIES) / Lothrop, Lee & Shepard (RIVERDALE STORIES).

See <u>Proud and lazy</u> (24) for compilation issued by Hurst.

Locations: DLC, FU, KU, MB, MWA, MiEM, MnU, MsHAu, Nh, NHD,
    NN, OAU, OBgU, OC, TxU, WM

022.   <u>Uncle Ben. A story for little folks.</u> Lee & Shepard,
       c1862. RIVERDALE STORIES v.5.

Copyright dated May 12, 1862, granted in the District of
Massachusetts to William T. Adams. Copy deposited October
18, 1864. Copyright renewal #7797 dated 1890, granted to
William T. Adams.

A small book designed for very young children.

Illustrations: Hammatt Billings; engraved by John Andrew.

Other Printings: Lee & Shepard (FLORA LEE STORY BOOKS v.2) /
    Lee & Shepard; Charles T. Dillingham (RIVERDALE STORIES) /
    Lothrop, Lee & Shepard (RIVERDALE STORIES).

See <u>The little merchant</u> (18) for compilation issued
by Hurst.

Locations: DLC, FU, MB, MWA, NHD, NN, OBgU, OC

023.   <u>The birthday party. A story for little folks.</u> Lee &
       Shepard, c1862. RIVERDALE STORIES v.6.

Copyright dated May 12, 1862, granted in the District of
Massachusetts to William T. Adams. Copy deposited October
18, 1864. Copyright renewal #7798 dated 1890, granted
to William T. Adams.

A small book designed for very young children.

Illustrations: Hammatt Billings; engraved by John Andrew.

023a. Poem entitled "Lizzie" on pp. 92-96.

Other Printings: Lee & Shepard (FLORA LEE STORY BOOKS v.3) /
    Lee & Shepard; Charles T. Dillingham (RIVERDALE STORIES) /
    Lothrop, Lee & Shepard (RIVERDALE STORIES).

See <u>Proud and lazy</u> (24) for compilation issued by Hurst.

Locations: CtY, CSmH, DLC, FU, IDekN, KU, MB, MWA, MsHAu,
    NHD, OBgU

024.   <u>Proud and lazy. A story for little folks.</u> Lee &
       Shepard, c1862. RIVERDALE STORIES v.7.

Copyright dated May 12, 1862, granted in the District of
Massachusetts to William T. Adams. Copy deposited October
18, 1864. Copyright renewal #7793 dated 1890, granted to
William T. Adams.

A small book designed for very young children.

Illustrations: Hammatt Billings; engraved by John Andrew.

Other Printings: Lee & Shepard (RIVERDALE STORY BOOKS v.4) /
Lee & Shepard; Charles T. Dillingham (RIVERDALE STORIES) /
Lothrop, Lee & Shepard (RIVERDALE STORIES).

A compilation entitled Proud and lazy was published by
Hurst on September 16, 1905.
Contents: Proud and lazy -- Careless Kate -- Dolly and I --
The birthday party. (see 21, 23, 25).
Hurst (HOME SERIES FOR GIRLS; OLIVER OPTIC BOOKS; RIVERDALE
STORIES).

Locations: CtY, DLC, FTS, FU, KU, MB, MWA, MiEM, MnU, MsHAu,
NHD, NN, OAU, OBgU, TxU, WM

Locations for Hurst compilation: FU, NN

025.   Careless Kate. A story for little folks. Lee & Shepard,
        c1862. RIVERDALE STORIES v.8.

Copyright dated May 12, 1862, granted in the District of
Massachusetts to William T. Adams. Copy deposited October
18, 1864. Copyright renewal #7799 dated 1890, granted
to William T. Adams.

A small book designed for very young children.

Illustrations: Hammatt Billings; engraved by John Andrew.

025a.   Poem entitled "Nothing to do" on pp. 89-96.

Other Printings: Lee & Shepard (RIVERDALE STORY BOOKS v.5) /
Lee & Shepard; Charles T. Dillingham (RIVERDALE STORIES) /
Lothrop, Lee & Shepard (RIVERDALE STORIES).

See Proud and lazy (24) for compilation issued by Hurst.

Locations: DLC, FTS, FU, MnU, MB, MWA, NHD, NN, PP, PPiU,
ViU, WM

026.   Robinson Crusoe, Jr. A story for little folks. Lee &
        Shepard, c1862. RIVERDALE STORIES v.9.

Copyright dated May 12, 1862, granted in the District of
Massachusetts to William T. Adams. Copy deposited October
18, 1864. Copyright renewal #7800 dated 1890, granted

to William T. Adams.

A small book designed for very young children.

Illustrations: Hammatt Billings; engraved by John Andrew.

Other Printings: Lee & Shepard (RIVERDALE STORY BOOKS v.6) /
    Lee & Shepard; Charles T. Dillingham (RIVERDALE STORIES) /
    Lothrop, Lee & Shepard (RIVERDALE STORIES).

See The do-somethings (29) for compilation issued by Hurst.

Locations: CtY, DLC, FTS, FU, KU, MB, MWA, MsHAu, NHD, NN,
    OBgU

027.   The picnic party. A story for little folks. Lee &
        Shepard, c1862. RIVERDALE STORIES v.10.

Copyright dated May 12, 1862, granted in the District of
Massachusetts to William T. Adams. Copy deposited October
18, 1864. Copyright renewal #7801 dated 1890, granted to
William T. Adams.

A small book designed for very young children.

Illustrations: Hammatt Billings; engraved by John Andrew.

Other Printings: Lee & Shepard (FLORA LEE STORY BOOKS v.4) /
    Lee & Shepard; Charles T. Dillingham (RIVERDALE STORIES) /
    Lothrop, Lee & Shepard (RIVERDALE STORIES).

See The do-somethings (29) for compilation issued by Hurst.

Locations: DLC, FTS, FU, MB, NHD, OAU, OBgU

028.   The gold thimble. A story for little folks. Lee &
        Shepard, c1862. RIVERDALE STORIES v.11.

Copyright dated May 12, 1862, granted in the District of
Massachusetts to William T. Adams. Copy deposited October
18, 1864. Copyright renewal #7802 dated 1890, granted
to William T. Adams.

A small book designed for very young children.

Illustrations: Hammatt Billings; engraved by John Andrew.

028a.   Poem entitled "Whip-poor-Will. A sad story of a naughty
        boy" on pp. 89-96.

Other Printings: Lee & Shepard (FLORA LEE STORY BOOKS v.5) /
    Lee & Shepard; Charles T. Dillingham (RIVERDALE STORIES) /
    Lothrop, Lee & Shepard (RIVERDALE STORIES).

See The little merchant (18) for compilation issued by
Hurst.

Locations: DLC, FTS, FU, IDekN, MB, MWA, MsHAu, NHD, Nh, OC,
   PP

029.   The do-somethings. A story for little folks. Lee &
       Shepard, c1862. RIVERDALE STORIES v.12.

Copyright dated May 12, 1862, granted in the District of
Massachusetts to William T. Adams. Copy deposited October
18, 1864. Copyright renewal #7803 dated 1890, granted to
William T. Adams.

A small book designed for very young children.

Illustrations: Hammatt Billings; engraved by John Andrew.

Other Printings: Lee & Shepard (FLORA LEE STORY BOOKS v.6) /
   Lee & Shepard; Charles T. Dillingham (RIVERDALE STORIES) /
   Lothrop, Lee & Shepard (RIVERDALE STORIES).

A compilation entitled The do-somethings was published by
Hurst on October 14, 1905.
Contents: The do-somethings -- The young voyagers --
Robinson Crusoe, Jr. -- The picnic party. (see 19, 26, 27).
Hurst (RIVERDALE STORIES; HOME SERIES FOR GIRLS).

Locations: DLC, FU, KU, MB, MWA, MWalB, MnU, NN, OBgU,
   PP, PPiU, WM

Locations for Hurst compilation: CtY, MiEM, MnU, NHD, PP

                              1863

030.   Sports and pastimes for indoors and out. With additions
       by Oliver Optic; embracing physical and intellectual
       amusements for young people, the family circle and
       evening parties. Containing acting, pantomine, and
       dialogue charades, anagrams, puzzles, conundrums,
       transpositions, games, magic, forfeits, chess,
       draughts, backgammon, gymnastics, fishing, skating,
       rowing, etc. G.W. Cottrell, c1863.

   This is a reprint of Parlour pastimes: a repertoire of
   acting charades, fire-side games, enigmas, riddles, etc.
   and Games for all seasons ...a sequel to "Parlour pastimes"
   by George F. Pardon. London, 1858.

Illustrations: Anonymous.

Locations: DLC, MB, NHD, OAU

031. "Live and learn: or, The adventures of Paul Clifford."

Appeared serially in The Student and Schoolmate, January - June 1863.

This title has not been located in book form.

032. A spelling book for advanced classes by William T. Adams. Brewer and Tileston, c1863.

Copyright dated February 24, 1863, granted in the District of Massachusetts. Copy deposited March 7, 1863. Copyright renewal #6033 dated April 17, 1880, granted to William T. Adams. Two copies deposited at LC on November 1, 1880.

Other Printings: William Ware / J.H. Butler.

Listed in "New Books Section" American Literary Gazette 1 (1 May 1863): 31.

Locations: DLC, MB, NHD, Nh

033. "Onward and upward: or, Paul Clifford in search of a situation."

Appeared serially in The Student and Schoolmate, July - December 1863.

Copyright dated September 19, 1863, granted in the District of Massachusetts. Copy deposited December 23, 1863.

This title not located in book form.

034. Rich and humble: or, The mission of Bertha Grant. A story for young people. Lee & Shepard, c1863. WOODVILLE STORIES v.1.

Copyright dated November 2, 1863, granted in the District of Massachusetts to William T. Adams. Copy deposited January 1, 1864. Copyright #25813 dated July 18, 1891, for renewal on November 2, 1891. Preface dated September 8, 1863.

Advertised as "New book, ready Saturday, November 21, 1863." American Literary Gazette 2 (1 December 1863): 107.

Illustrations: W.L. Champney; engraved by Samuel S. Kilburn and Richard L. Mallory.

Reviews: "No author is more welcomed by the young, and no books can be more safely placed in their hands. His writings, as in this volume of 'Rich and Humble,' inspire

the reader with a lofty purpose. They show the wrong
courses of life only to present, by contrast, the true
and right path, and make it the way which youth will
wish to walk in, because of its being the most pleasant
and inviting." Mass. Teacher. [per L&S ad].

Other Printings: Burt / Conkey / Donohue (OLIVER OPTIC
    SERIES #12) / Hurst (CAMBRIDGE CLASSICS; LAURELHURST
    SERIES; OLIVER OPTIC BOOKS; YOUNG AMERICA LIBRARY FOR
    BOYS) / Lee & Shepard (AMERICAN BOYS' SERIES #33) /
    Lee & Shepard; Charles T. Dillingham (WOODVILLE STORIES) /
    Lippincott / Lothrop, Lee & Shepard (AMERICAN BOYS' SERIES
    #33; OLIVER OPTIC SERIES #19; WOODVILLE STORIES) / New
    York Book Co. (OLIVER OPTIC BOOKS) / Street & Smith
    (ALGER SERIES #130; MEDAL LIBRARY #333).

Variant Titles: Rich and humble: or, Life's best gift.
    (ALGER SERIES).

Locations: CtY, DLC, FTS, FU, GEU, IDekN, KU, MB, MWA, MWalB,
    MnU, MsHAu, NHD, NN, Nh, OAU, OBgU, OC, PP, TxU, ViU, WM

*035.   In school and out: or, The conquest of Richard Grant. A
        story for young people. Lee & Shepard, c1863.
        WOODVILLE STORIES v.2.

Copyright dated November 2, 1863, granted in the District
of Massachusetts. Copy deposited January 1, 1864. Copyright #25814 dated July 18, 1891 for renewal on November
2, 1891. Preface dated October 26, 1863.

Description: "Oliver Optic is as well known and as highly
    appreciated among the young people of our land as Charles
    Dickens is among the older folks. 'In School and Out' is
    equal to anything he has written. It is a story that will
    deeply interest boys particularly, and make them better."
    Notices of the Press. [per L&S ad].

Illustrations: W.L. Champney.

Reviews: "This is a good, hearty, vigorous, muscular story,
    telling us how an adventurous and impulsive youth tumbled
    out of one scrape into another, until at last his better
    nature won a victory over the foe in his heart, and he
    made a man of himself...Mr. Adams' juveniles leave a
    healthy impression; and he has a way of working his moral
    into the narrative without obtruding it so palpably that
    it acts sometimes rather as a scarecrow." American
    Literary Gazette octavo series 2 (15 January 1864): 214-15.

    Advertised as "Ready December 11, 1863." American
    Literary Gazette 2 (1 December 1863): 107.

Other Printings: Burt / Conkey / Donohue (BOYS BANNER SERIES
    #4; OLIVER OPTIC SERIES #7) / Hurst (CAMBRIDGE CLASSICS;

LAURELHURST SERIES; OLIVER OPTIC BOOKS; YOUNG AMERICA
LIBRARY FOR BOYS) / Lee & Shepard (AMERICAN BOYS' SERIES
#23) / Lee & Shepard; Lee, Shepard & Dillingham (WOODVILLE
STORIES) / Lothrop, Lee & Shepard (AMERICAN BOYS' SERIES
#23; OLIVER OPTIC SERIES #20; WOODVILLE STORIES) / New
York Book Co. (OLIVER OPTIC BOOKS) / Street & Smith
(ALGER SERIES #131; MEDAL LIBRARY #339).

Variant Titles: In school and out: or, Happy days. (ALGER
SERIES); In school and out: or, A story for wide-awake
boys. (MEDAL LIBRARY); In school and out: or, A tale for
wide-awake boys. (Donohue).

Locations: CtY, DLC, FTS, FU, KU, MB, MWA, MWalB, MiEM, MnU,
MsHAu, NHD, NN, Nh, OAU, OBgU, OC, PP, PPiU, WM

036. The soldier boy: or, Tom Somers in the Army. A story of
      the great rebellion. Lee & Shepard, c1863. ARMY AND
      NAVY STORIES v.1.

Copyright dated November 24, 1863, granted in the District
of Massachusetts to William T. Adams. Copy deposited June
27, 1864. Copyright renewal #43904 dated October 2, 1893.
Preface dated February 22, 1864.

Illustrations: W.L. Champney; engraved by John Andrew.

Reviews: "This is a story of the rebellion, narrating the
      adventures of a patriotic youth, who left the comforts of
      home to share the dangers of the field. He is carried
      through several battles, and for a while shared the
      hospitalities of the rebels as a prisoner. The story
      is true to history, giving in the form of personal
      adventure correct accounts of many stirring scenes of the
      war." Hartford Courant. [per L&S ad].

      "Decidedly the best story of the Rebellion which has yet
      been published...It is the record of the experience of
      one of those gallant fellows who went to the war in the
      ranks of our grand army. The hero was taken prisoner at
      Bull Run, escaped from the rebels, and through many perils
      made his way over the Blue Ridge and down the Shenandoah,
      captured a schooner at Budd's Ferry, and was promoted for
      gallant conduct at Williamsburg. His adventures are full
      of life and spirit and will enchain the attention of the
      reader. [L&S ad] in American Literary Gazette 5 (1 July
      1865): 109.

Other Printings: Burt / Donohue (OLIVER OPTIC SERIES #14) /
      Hurst (OLIVER OPTIC BOOKS) / Lee & Shepard (AMERICAN BOYS'
      SERIES #53; SOLDIER BOY SERIES v.1) / Lee & Shepard;
      Charles T. Dillingham (ARMY AND NAVY STORIES) / Lothrop,
      Lee & Shepard (AMERICAN BOYS' SERIES #53; ARMY AND NAVY
      STORIES; OLIVER OPTIC SERIES #1; SOLDIER BOY SERIES v.1).

Locations: CSmH, CtY, DLC, FTS, FU, GEU, IDekN, KU, MB, MWA,
    MWalB, MiEM, MnU, MoS, MsHaU, NHD, NN, Nh, OAU, OC, PP,
    PPiU, TxU

037. The sailor boy: or, Jack Somers in the Navy. A story
      of the great rebellion. Lee & Shepard, c1863.
      ARMY AND NAVY STORIES v.2.

    Copyright dated November 24, 1863, granted in the District
    of Massachusetts to William T. Adams. Copy deposited
    January 4, 1865. Copyright renewal #43903 dated October 2,
    1893. Preface dated November 24, 1864. New preface dated
    April 1893.

Illustrations: Anonymous; engraved by Nathan Brown.

Reviews: "Jack is the brother of Tom, the Soldier Boy, whose
    adventures in the army were so much enjoyed. We have
    only to repeat that there are few better stories for boys
    than these of Mr. Adams'. Always bright and sparkling
    with animation, the story never drags; there are no stupid
    tasks or tiresome descriptions; the boys whose characters
    are drawn are real boys, impulsive, with superabundant
    animal life, and the heroes are manly, generous, healthy
    creations." Hartford Press. [per L&S ad].

    "...It is described as not altogether a romance, but as a
    judicious blending of fact and fiction, the former largely
    predominating. The scene of operations referred to is
    chiefly that of the Western Gulf Squadron." American
    Literary Gazette 4 (16 January 1865): 167-68.

    "'Jack' is the brother of 'Tom, the Soldier Boy,' and
    his adventures on the sea will be found to be as thrilling
    and wonderful as those of his brother on the land. The
    descriptions of general engagements and sea-life are
    trustworthy, facts being connected by a thread of fiction
    to give more continuity and interest to the story."
    American Literary Gazette 5 (1 July 1865): 109.

  Other Printings: Burt / Donohue (OLIVER OPTIC SERIES #13) /
    Hurst (OLIVER OPTIC BOOKS) / Lee & Shepard (SAILOR BOY
    SERIES v.1) / Lee & Shepard; Charles T. Dillingham (ARMY
    AND NAVY STORIES) / Lothrop, Lee & Shepard (ARMY AND NAVY
    STORIES; OLIVER OPTIC SERIES #4; SAILOR BOY SERIES v.1) /
    Street & Smith (ALGER SERIES #165; MEDAL LIBRARY #375).

Locations: CSmH, CtY, DLC, FTS, FU, IDekN, KU, MB, MWA,
    MWalB, MiEM, MnU, MoS, MsHaU, NHD, NN, Nh, OAU, OBgU,
    OC, PP, PPiU, TxU, ViU

                        1864

038. "Trials and triumphs: or, Paul Clifford in trouble."

Appeared serially in The Student and Schoolmate,
January - June 1864.

This title has not been located in book form.

039.   "Work and play: or, Paul Clifford's vacation."

Appeared serially in The Student and Schoolmate,
July - December 1864.

This title has not been located in book form.

040.   Watch and wait: or, The young fugitives. A story for
        young people.   Lee & Shepard, c1864. WOODVILLE
        STORIES v.3.

Copyright dated September 27, 1864, granted in the
District of Massachusetts. Copy deposited February 11(?),
1865. Copyright #18303X dated April 27, 1892 for renewal
on September 27, 1892. Preface dated August 15, 1864.

Advertised as "Will be ready early in September."
American Literary Gazette 3 (15 September 1864): 315.

Illustrations: Anonymous.

Reviews: "The author has used, to the best advantage, the
    many exciting incidents that naturally attend the career
    of a fugitive slave, and the seeds that he may sow in
    youthful hearts will perhaps bear a hundred-fold."
    [per L&S ad].

    "...It has the graphic merit that belongs to all the other
    volumes of the series, and is to be regarded as a contri-
    bution to the juvenile department of our anti-slavery
    literature. Although, madams, the author says he 'is
    forced to acknowledge that his book was not written in
    the interests of the anti-slavery cause,' yet he adds,
    'if the story shall kindle any new emotion of sympathy
    for the oppressed and enslaved, it will have more than
    answered the purpose for which it was intended.'"
    American Literary Gazette 3 (15 October 1864): 386.

Other Printings: Burt / Donohue (OLIVER OPTIC SERIES #17) /
    Hurst (OLIVER OPTIC BOOKS; YOUNG AMERICA LIBRARY FOR BOYS)
    / Lee & Shepard (AMERICAN BOYS' SERIES #43) / Lothrop, Lee
    & Shepard (AMERICAN BOYS' SERIES #43; OLIVER OPTIC SERIES
    #21; WOODVILLE STORIES) / Street & Smith (ALGER SERIES
    #132; MEDAL LIBRARY #315).

Locations: CtY, DLC, FTS, FU, KU, MB, MWA, MWalB, MiEM, MnU,
    MoS, NHD, NN, Nh, OAU, OBgU, OC, PP, TxU, ViU

1865

041. "Out in the world: or, Paul Clifford on a cruise."

Appeared serially in The Student and Schoolmate, January - December 1865.

This title has not been located in book form.

042. The young lieutenant: or, The adventures of an Army officer. A story of the great rebellion. Lee & Shepard, c1865. ARMY AND NAVY STORIES v.3.

Copyright dated June 12, 1865, granted in the District of Massachusetts to William T. Adams. Copy deposited June 13, 1865. Copyright #3269 dated April 24, 1893, for renewal on June 12, 1893. Preface undated.

Illustrations: Anonymous; engraved by John Andrew.

Reviews: "This volume is a continuation of the adventures of 'Tom Somers,' after receiving his commission as lieutenant and donning the 'shoulder straps' and is equally interesting and exciting, introducing new characters and scenes, perilous adventures and novel situations. The battles of Glendale and Malvern Hills, adventures in the enemy's camp, 'Up Chimney,' 'Down Drain,' and 'In Petersburg,' &c. are among the lively and exciting subjects of this truthful narrative of a soldier's life." American Literary Gazette 5 (1 July 1865): 109.

Other Printings: Burt / Donohue (OLIVER OPTIC SERIES #20) / Hurst (OLIVER OPTIC BOOKS; YOUNG AMERICA LIBRARY FOR BOYS) / Lee & Shepard (SOLDIER BOY SERIES v.2) / Lee & Shepard; Charles T. Dillingham (ARMY AND NAVY STORIES) / Lee & Shepard; Lee, Shepard & Dillingham (ARMY AND NAVY STORIES) / Lothrop, Lee & Shepard (ARMY AND NAVY STORIES; OLIVER OPTIC SERIES #2; SOLDIER BOY SERIES v.2) / Saalfield.

Locations: CSmH, CtY, DLC, FTS, FU, GEU, IDekN, MB, MWA, MWalB, MiEM, MnU, MsHAL, NHD, NN, Nh, OAU, OBgU, OC, PP, PPiU, TxU, ViU

043. "The cruise of the Leopold: or, The fortunes of a good-for-nothing."

Appeared serially in Our Young Folks v.1 #10-12 (October - December 1865).

This title has not been located in book form.

044.   The Yankee middy: or, The adventures of a naval officer.
       A story of the great rebellion.   Lee & Shepard, c1865.
       ARMY AND NAVY STORIES v.4.

       Copyright dated November 20, 1865, granted in the District
       of Massachusetts to William T. Adams.   Copy deposited
       March 12, 1866.   Copyright #16658 dated August 9, 1893,
       for renewal on November 20, 1893.   Preface dated October
       23, 1865.

Illustrations: Charles A. Barry.

Reviews: "The incidents of the story are those which have
       occurred on the ocean, and on the bays, inlets, and rivers
       of the South, common in the experience of all our naval
       officers who have been actively employed during the war."
       Notices of the Press. [per L&S ad].

       "Mr. Adams, although a prolific writer, is nevertheless, a
       capital writer of juveniles..."   American Literary Gazette
       6 (15 December 1865): 132.

       "Mr. Adams has written many books for boys that have
       deserved and obtained popularity.   The present work seems
       fully equal to its predecessors in clearness and interest
       and agrees also with them in being superior in composition
       to the average tales for the same class of readers."
       Nation 1 (14 December 1865): 757.

Other Printings: Burt / Donohue (OLIVER OPTIC SERIES #19) /
       Hurst (OLIVER OPTIC BOOKS; YOUNG AMERICA LIBRARY FOR BOYS)
       / Lee & Shepard (SAILOR BOY SERIES v.2) / Lee & Shepard;
       Lee, Shepard & Dillingham (ARMY AND NAVY STORIES) /
       Lothrop, Lee & Shepard (ARMY AND NAVY STORIES; OLIVER
       OPTIC SERIES #5; SAILOR BOY SERIES v.2) / Street & Smith
       (ALGER SERIES #166; NEW MEDAL LIBRARY #382).

Variant Titles: The Yankee middy: or, True to his colors.
       (ALGER SERIES).

Locations: CSmH, CtY, DLC, FTS, FU, IDekN, KU, MB, MWA, MWalB,
       MiEM, MnU, MsHAu, NHD, NN, Nh, OAU, OC, PP, TxU, ViU, WM

045.   Work and win: or, Noddy Newman on a cruise. A story for
       young people.   Lee & Shepard, c1865. WOODVILLE
       STORIES v.4.

       Copyright dated November 20, 1865, granted in the District
       of Massachusetts to William T. Adams.   Copy deposited
       March 12, 1866.   Copyright #16659 dated August 9, 1893
       for renewal on November 20, 1893.   Preface undated.

       Advertised as "Now ready."   American Literary Gazette 6
       (15 November 1865): 70.

Illustrations: W.L. Champney.

Reviews: "A nautical story of adventure and endurance,
    written to delineate the upward progress of a boy whose
    moral attributes were of the lowest order, in consequence
    of neglected education, but in whom high religious princi-
    ples were afterwards developed." Notices of the Press.
    [per L&S ad].

    "Oliver Optic continues his Woodville Stories with 'Work
    and Win.' The moral which is conveyed in the text is
    revealed by Mr. Adams in his preface, which parents may
    read and the boys and girls skip if they please." Nation
    1 (28 December 1865): 818.

Other Printings: Burt / Donohue (OLIVER OPTIC SERIES #18) /
    Hurst (OLIVER OPTIC BOOKS; YOUNG AMERICA LIBRARY FOR
    BOYS) / Lee & Shepard (AMERICAN BOYS' SERIES #47) / Lee &
    Shepard; Lee, Shepard & Dillingham (WOODVILLE STORIES) /
    Lothrop, Lee & Shepard (AMERICAN BOYS' SERIES #47; OLIVER
    OPTIC SERIES #22; WOODVILLE STORIES) / New York Book Co.
    (OLIVER OPTIC BOOKS) / Street & Smith (ALGER SERIES #133;
    MEDAL LIBRARY #311].

Variant Titles: Work and win: or, The best way to succeed.
    (ALGER SERIES).

Locations: CSmH, CtY, DLC, FTS, FU, GEU, IDekN, KU, MB, MWA,
    MWalB, MnU, MsHAu, NHD, NN, Nh, OAU, OBgU, OC, PP

046. Fighting Joe: or, The fortunes of a staff officer. A
      story of the great rebellion. Lee & Shepard, c1865.
      ARMY AND NAVY STORIES v.5.

    Copyright dated December 20, 1865, granted in the District
    of Massachusetts to William T. Adams. Copy deposited
    March 12, 1866. Copyright #16660 dated August 9, 1893,
    for renewal on December 20, 1893. Preface undated.

Illustrations: W.L. Champney.

Reviews: "The description of battles and sieges, of picket and
    skirmishing, of camp life and marching, are wrought out
    with thrilling detail, making the story truly fascinating;
    while, in connection with this, useful and practical
    information respecting men and places is conveyed, and a
    proper spirit of morality and patriotism inculcated."
    Notices of the Press. [per L&S ad].

Other Printings: Burt / Donohue (OLIVER OPTIC SERIES #4) /
    Hurst (OLIVER OPTIC BOOKS; YOUNG AMERICA LIBRARY FOR BOYS)
    / Lee & Shepard (SAILOR BOY SERIES v.3) / Lee & Shepard;
    Charles T. Dillingham (ARMY AND NAVY STORIES) / Lothrop,
    Lee & Shepard (ARMY AND NAVY STORIES; OLIVER OPTIC SERIES
    #3; SOLDIER BOY SERIES v.3) / New York Book Co. (OLIVER

OPTIC BOOKS).

Locations: CSmH, CtY, DLC, FTS, FU, GEU, IDekN, KU, MB, MWA,
   MWalB, MiEM, MnU, MsHAu, NHD, Nh, OAU, OBgU, OC, PP, TxU,
   ViU, WM

1866

047. "The club boat: or, The fairy archers of Islington."

Appeared serially in The Student and Schoolmate,
January - December 1866.

This title has not been located in book form.

048. Brave Old Salt: or, Life on the quarter deck. A story
   of the great rebellion. Lee & Shepard, c1866. ARMY
   AND NAVY STORIES v.6.

Copyright dated March 28, 1866, granted in the District
of Massachusetts to William T. Adams. Copy deposited
May 12(?), 1866. Preface dated March 13, 1866.

Illustrations: Anonymous.

Reviews: "A book of adventure, of personal experience,
   describing a living hero, and exhibiting the great truth
   that, by fidelity of conscience, country, and God, earthly
   and heavenly blessings are secured." [L&S ad].

Other Printings: Burt / Donohue (OLIVER OPTIC SERIES #2) /
   Hurst (OLIVER OPTIC BOOKS; YOUNG AMERICA LIBRARY FOR BOYS)
   / Lee & Shepard (SAILOR BOY SERIES v.3) / Lee & Shepard;
   Charles T. Dillingham (ARMY AND NAVY STORIES) / Lee &
   Shepard; Lee, Shepard & Dillingham (ARMY AND NAVY STORIES)
   / Lothrop, Lee & Shepard (ARMY AND NAVY STORIES; OLIVER
   OPTIC SERIES #6; SAILOR BOY SERIES v.3) / Street & Smith
   (ALGER SERIES #167; NEW MEDAL LIBRARY #387) / Ward & Lock.

Variant Titles: Brave Old Salt: or, The boy they could not
   down. (ALGER SERIES).

Locations: CSmH, CtY, DLC, FTS, FU, GEU, IDekN, KU, MB, MWA,
   MWalB, MnU, MoS, MsHAu, NHD, NN, Nh, OAU, OBgU, OC, PP,
   PPiU, ViU, WM

049. Hope and have: or, Fanny Grant among the Indians. A
   story for young people. Lee & Shepard, c1866.
   WOODVILLE STORIES v.5.

Copyright dated October 3, 1866, granted in the District
of Massachusetts to William T. Adams. Copy deposited
October 23, 1866. Copyright #19506 dated July 10, 1894

for renewal on October 3, 1894.   Preface dated July 16,
1866.

Illustrations: W.L. Champney.

Reviews: "This is a story of Western adventure and of peril
   among the Indians, and contains the experience of Fanny
   Grant, who, from a very naughty girl, became a very good
   one, by the influence of a pure and beautiful example
   exhibited by an erring child, in the hour of her greatest
   wandering from the path of virtue." Philadelphia Age.
   [per L&S ad].

Other Printings: Donohue (OLIVER OPTIC SERIES #6) / Hurst /
   Lee & Shepard (AMERICAN BOYS' SERIES #22) / Lee & Shepard;
   Lee, Shepard & Dillingham (WOODVILLE STORIES) / Lothrop,
   Lee & Shepard (AMERICAN BOYS' SERIES #22; OLIVER OPTIC
   SERIES #23; WOODVILLE STORIES) / New York Book Co. (OLIVER
   OPTIC BOOKS) / Street & Smith (ALGER SERIES #134; MEDAL
   LIBRARY #179).

Variant Titles: Hope and have: or, On his own resources.
   (ALGER SERIES).

Locations: CtY, DLC, FTS, FU, GEU, KU, MB, MWA, MWalB, MiEM,
   MnU, MoS, MsHAu, NHD, NN, Nh, OAU, OBgU, OC, PP, TxU

050. Haste and waste: or, The young pilot of Lake Champlain.
      A story for young people.   Lee & Shepard, c1866.
      WOODVILLE STORIES v.6.

Copyright dated October 3, 1866, granted in the District
of Massachusetts to William T. Adams.   Copy deposited
October 23, 1866.   Copyright #19505 dated July 10, 1894
for renewal on October 3, 1894.   Preface undated.

Illustrations: Anonymous.

Reviews: "This is a story of boyish daring and integrity upon
   Lake Champlain, and older heads than those of sixteen may
   read and profit by it." [L&S ad].

Other Printings: Donohue (OLIVER OPTIC SERIES #5) / Hurst /
   Lee & Shepard (AMERICAN BOYS' SERIES #21) / Lee & Shepard;
   Lee, Shepard & Dillingham (WOODVILLE STORIES) / Lothrop,
   Lee & Shepard (AMERICAN BOYS' SERIES #21; OLIVER OPTIC
   SERIES #24; WOODVILLE STORIES) / New York Book Co. (OLIVER
   OPTIC BOOKS) / Street & Smith (ALGER SERIES #135; MEDAL
   LIBRARY #174).

Variant Titles: Haste and waste: or, The result of
   indifference.   (ALGER SERIES).

Locations: CtY, CSmH, DLC, FTS, FU, IDekN, KU, MB, MWA, MWalB,
   MiEM, MnU, MsHAu, NHD, NN, Nh, OBgU, OC, PP, WM

051. Outward bound: or, Young America afloat. A story of
      travel and adventure by William T. Adams. Lee &
      Shepard, c1866. YOUNG AMERICA ABROAD 1st series v.1.

      Copyright dated November 22, 1866, granted in the District
      of Massachusetts to William T. Adams. Copy deposited
      January 1, 1867. Copyright #19507, dated July 10, 1894
      for renewal on November 22, 1894. Preface dated November
      2, 1866.

      Advertised as "Ready in November [1866]." American
      Literary Gazette 8 (1 November 1866).

Description: "...The Ship Young America, sails for Europe,
      with a school of eighty-seven boys aboard her, who pursue
      the studies of a school, and at the same time work the
      ship across the Atlantic, being amenable to regular naval
      discipline." [L&S ad].

Illustrations: Anonymous; engraved by Samuel S. Kilburn.

Reviews: "[Outward bound] will make the eyes of the author's
      numerous young friends to sparkle with delight. It is the
      first volume of 'A Library of Travel and Adventure in
      Foreign Lands,' and contains the narrative of the voyage
      of the Academy ship 'Young America' across the waters..."
      Hours at Home 6 (April 1868): 571.

      " So long as there are principals of academies we suppose
      books by 'Oliver Optic' will be sold in great numbers.
      The schoolmaster must feel a peculiar pleasure, the
      pleasure of 'adding his sum of more to that which had' a
      great plenty, in giving a book like 'Outward Bound' to an
      exemplary pupil of high rank in his classes. For Mr.
      Adams never forgets that he is a schoolmaster. His model
      man is always firm, but kindly, inflexibly just, and never
      in the wrong. The boys always find that he knew best, and
      had a good reason for every rule. And good the boys are
      always, manly and honorable and scorn to deceive their
      instructor, and even the prop-shaker and apple-stealer
      generally knocks under in the last chapter and confesses
      that his teacher has been his best friend..." Nation 3
      (20 December 1866): 492-93.

Other Printings: Donohue (OLIVER OPTIC SERIES #10) / Hurst /
      Lee & Shepard (AMERICAN BOYS' SERIES #52) / Lee & Shepard;
      Lee, Shepard & Dillingham (YOUNG AMERICA ABROAD) / Log
      Cabin Press (LOG CABIN LIBRARY - LOG CABIN SERIES #16) /
      Lothrop, Lee & Shepard (AMERICAN BOYS' SERIES #52; OLIVER
      OPTIC SERIES #35; YOUNG AMERICA ABROAD) / MacLellan
      (MACLELLAN BOOKS) / Superior Printing Co. (THE SUPERIOR
      LIBRARY).

Locations: CtY, CSmH, DLC, FTS, FU, IDekN, KU, MB, MWA, MWalB,
      MiEM, MnU, MoS, MsHAu, NHD, NN, Nh, OAU, OBgU, OC, PP, TxU,
      ViU

052.   The way of the world. A novel by William T. Adams.
        Lee & Shepard, c1866.

        Copyright dated November 24, 1866, granted in the District
        of Massachusetts to William T. Adams. Copy deposited Jan-
        uary 1, 1867. Copyright #19508 dated July 10, 1894, for
        renewal on November 22, 1894.

Reviews: "This story treats of a fortune of $3,000,000, left
        a youthful heir. The volume comprises 464 pages, and
        bears evidence in every chapter of the fresh, original
        and fascinating style which has always enlivened Mr.
        Adams's productions. We have the same felicitous manner
        of working out the plot by conversation, the same quaint
        wit and humor, and a class of characters which stand out
        boldly, pen photographs of living beings..." [L&S ad].

        Also reviewed in Daily Picayune 9 (June 1872): 9; Godey's
        85 (August 1872): 187; Godey's 121 (December 1890): 542.

Other Printings: Lee & Shepard (THE HOUSEHOLD LIBRARY v.3) /
        Lee & Shepard; Lee, Shepard & Dillingham / Research
        Publications (WRIGHT AMERICAN FICTION v.2 [1851-1875]
        reel A-4 no.27).

        Also published with title Three millions! or, The way of
        the world (53).

References: Wright II, #27.

Locations: CSmH, CtY, DLC, FTS, MB, MWA, MnU, NHD, NN, OAU,
        ViU

053.   Three millions! or, The way of the world by William T.
        Adams. Lee & Shepard, c1866.

        This is the same story as The way of the world (52).

Other Printings: Donohue (OLIVER OPTIC SERIES #15) / Lee &
        Shepard (GOOD COMPANY SERIES v.3) / Lothrop, Lee &
        Shepard.

Locations: DLC

                              1867

054.   Oliver Optic's magazine: our boys and girls.

        Edited by Oliver Optic January 1867 - December 1875.

Dates: January 1867 - December 1875 (vol.1 #1 - vol.18 #269).
Editors: William Taylor Adams (1867-1875).
Publisher: Lee & Shepard (1867-1875).
References: R. Gordon Kelly. Children's periodicals of the

United States. Westport, CT: Greenwood Press, 1983.
Betty L. Lyons. "A history of children's magazines published in the United States from 1789-1899. (Ph.D. dissertation, Johns Hopkins University, 1942).

Frequent Contributors: Rosa Abbott, George M. Baker, James
    DeMille, Amanda Douglas, Julia Ward Howe, Elijah Kellogg,
    Olive Logan, May Mannering, Sophie May, Louise Chandler
    Moulton, Oliver Optic, E.A. Samuels, and Wirt Sikes.

Frequent Illustrators: Charles G. Bush, W.L. Champney, Felix
    O.C. Darley, Lisbeth B. Humphrey, Thomas Nast, and Henry
    L. Stephens.

Features: Serialized stories by Oliver Optic and others were
    a main feature of the magazine. Departments included:
    "Dialogues;" "The Orator," which contained elocution
    lessons complete with appropriate gestures; "The Play-
    ground," which discussed sports for boys; "Headwork,"
    contained puzzles, rebuses and riddles, many contributed
    by the readers; "Pigeon-Hole Papers" and "Our Letter
    Bag" both contained correspondence.

Other Information: Adams wrote one serialized story for each
    volume. These stories were later published as full length
    books. See entries 55-58, 61, 62, 64, 66, 68-71, 74-77,
    79, 81, 82, 84, 87, 89, 91, 92, 96, 98.

    Adams frequently used the editorial columns to defend
    himself and his writings. His most famous and persistent
    critics were Louisa May Alcott, Emily Huntington Miller,
    Edward Eggleston, and Thomas Wentworth Higginson.

Locations: CSmH, CtY, DLC, FTS, FU, KU, MB, MWA, MiEM, MsHAu,
    NN, NhD, OC, PPiU, WM

Items 54a - 541 are reprints of some of the volumes of Oliver
    Optic's Magazine.

054a. Our boys and girls storyteller. Containing stories of
           the sea, tales of wonder, records of travel,
           anecdotes of natural history, wonderful things,
           dialogues, puzzles, &c.

    Reprint of Oliver Optic's Magazine v.1 (January - June
    1867).

Locations: FU

054b. Our boys and girls favorite.

    Advertised in American Literary Gazette 18 (December 1871).

054c. Our boys and girls companion.

Reprint of <u>Oliver Optic's Magazine</u> v.5 (January - June 1869).

Locations: DLC

054d.   <u>Our boys and girls treasure.</u>

Reprint of <u>Oliver Optic's Magazine</u> v.6 (July - December 1869).

Locations: DLC

054e.   <u>Our boys and girls repository.</u>

Reprint of <u>Oliver Optic's Magazine</u> v.7 (January - June 1870).

Locations: DLC

054f.   <u>Our boys and girls keepsake.</u>

Reprint of <u>Oliver Optic's Magazine</u> v.8 (July - December 1870).

Locations: DLC

054g.   <u>Our boys and girls album.</u>

Reprint of <u>Oliver Optic's Magazine</u> v.9 (January - June 1871).

Locations: DLC

054h.   <u>Our boys and girls museum.</u>

Reprint of <u>Oliver Optic's Magazine</u> v.10 (July - December 1871).

Locations: DLC

054i.   <u>Our boys and girls cabinet.</u>

Reprint of <u>Oliver Optic's Magazine</u> v.11 (January - June 1872).

Locations: DLC

054j.   <u>Our boys and girls mirror.</u>

Reprint of <u>Oliver Optic's Magazine</u> v.12 (July - December 1872).

Locations: DLC

054k. <u>Our boys and girls offering.</u>

Reprint of <u>Oliver Optic's Magazine</u> v.17 (January - June 1875).

054l. <u>Our boys and girls souvenir.</u>

Reprint of <u>Oliver Optic's Magazine</u> v.18 (July - December 1875).

Locations: FU, MWA, MiEM

055.   <u>The starry flag: or, The young fisherman of Cape Ann.</u>
       Lee & Shepard, c1867.   STARRY FLAG SERIES v.1.

Originally appeared serially in <u>Oliver Optic's Magazine</u> v.1 #1-26 (5 January - 29 June 1867).

Copyright dated October 14, 1867, granted in the District of Massachusetts to William T. Adams. Copy deposited October 14, 1867. Copyright #26955 dated May 17, 1895, for renewal on October 14, 1895. Preface dated September 17, 1867.

Advertised as "Just published." <u>American Literary Gazette</u> 10 (1 November 1867): 31.

Description: "...Although this story is mainly fiction, it is not without a foundation of truth, both in the relations of the hero to his uncle, and in the singular event upon which the turning-point of the plot rests...It is more important that the hero should be worthy of the admiration and regard of the reader...the author hopes that his young friends, while they strive to be as resolute and daring as Levi, will also endeavor to be as noble and true, as void of offence before God and man, as he labored to be..." [preface].

Illustrations: Granville Perkins; engraved by Samuel S. Kilburn.

Reviews: "The early history of Levi Fairfield, the boy hero of this volume, as it is graphically traced by Oliver Optic, will be apt to hold boy-readers spellbound. His manly virtue, his determined character, his superiority to mean vice, his industry, and his stirring adventures, will suggest good lessons for imitation." <u>Presbyterian.</u> [per L&S ad].

Other Printings: Lee & Shepard (AMERICAN BOYS' SERIES #54) /
    Lee & Shepard; Charles T. Dillingham (STARRY FLAG SERIES)
    / Lothrop, Lee & Shepard (OLIVER OPTIC SERIES #25; STARRY
    FLAG SERIES) / Street & Smith (ALGER SERIES #153; NEW
    MEDAL LIBRARY #393).

Variant Titles: The starry flag: or, A splendid adventure.
    (ALGER SERIES).

Locations: CtY, DLC, FTS, FU, KU, MB, MWA, MWalB, MiEM, MnU,
    MsHAu, NHD, NM, Nh, CBgU, OC, PP, PPiU, WM

056. Breaking away: or, The fortunes of a student. Lee &
        Shepard, c1867. STARRY FLAG SERIES v.2.

Originally appeared serially in Oliver Optic's Magazine
v.2 #27-39 (6 July - 28 September 1867).

Copyright dated October 29, 1867, granted in the District
of Massachusetts. Copy deposited December 31, 1867.
Copyright #26957 dated May 7, 1895, for renewal on October
29, 1895. Preface dated September 23, 1867.

Advertised as "To be issued shortly." American Literary
Gazette 10 (1 November 1867): 31.

Illustrations: Thomas Nast; engraved by Samuel S. Kilburn.

Reviews: "In this volume Oliver Optic opens the school-room
    door, and shows the nature, construction, and workings of
    the school system; its lights and shadows; its discipline,
    and the serious consequences that come from want of
    discipline." Patriot. [per L&S ad].

    "In this volume are described the adventures of the pupils
    of the Parkville Liberal Institute, consequent on their
    revolt against a tyrannical principal. Their 'treasons,
    stratagems, and spoils' are told in pleasing style and
    will meet none the less with boyish approval if somewhat
    difficult of imitation." Catholic World 6 (January 1868):
    575.

Other Printings: Lee & Snepard; Lee, Shepard & Dillingham
    (STARRY FLAG SERIES) / Lothrop, Lee & Shepard (OLIVER
    OPTIC SERIES #26; STARRY FLAG SERIES) / Street & Smith
    (ALGER SERIES #154; NEW MEDAL LIBRARY #397).

Variant Titles: Breaking away: or, Pluck brings luck.
    (ALGER SERIES).

Locations: CSmH, CtY, DLC, FTS, FU, IDekN, KU, MB, MWA, MiEM,
    MnU, NHD, NN, OAU, OC, PP, TxU, WM

057. The voyage of life: an allegory by Oliver Optic and

George M. Baker.

Originally appeared serially in Oliver Optic's Magazine
v.2 #32-33 (10 - 17 August 1867).

Copyright #26980 dated October 19, 1887, granted to Walter
H. Baker Co. Two copies deposited at LC on October 27,
1887.

Published in book form by Walter H. Baker Co.

Locations: DLC

058.   Seek and find: or, The adventures of a smart boy.   Lee &
        Shepard, c1867. STARRY FLAG SERIES v.3.

Originally appeared serially in Oliver Optic's Magazine
v.2 #40-52 (5 October - 28 December 1867).

Copyright dated December 3, 1867, granted in the District
of Massachusetts to William T. Adams. Copy deposited
December 31, 1867. Copyright #35910 dated July 10, 1895
for renewal on December 3, 1895. Preface dated November
29, 1867.

Advertised as "Ready in December [1867]." American
Literary Gazette 10 (1 November 1867): 31.

Description: "Earnest Thornton, the 'smart boy' of this
    story, is a clear headed, well intentioned, plucky boy,
    that has a high aim and means right even where he is
    wrong, and his adventures will be read with interest."
    [L&S ad].

Illustrations: Granville Perkins; engraved by Samuel S.
    Kilburn.

Reviews: "Lee & Shepard are still delighting our young folks
    with their issues, among the last of which we note: Seek
    and Find..." Hours At Home 6 (February 1868): 384.

    "The facility with which 'Oliver Optic' turns out books
    for boys would be something wonderful and commendable if
    the books were at all hard to make or good when made; but
    they are all very poor...If we could have our way, the
    sale of them should stop immediately and entirely...Such
    books, whatever Mr. Adams and the poor children may think,
    are worse than worthless. They encourage youthful impu-
    dence and 'smartness,' and do nothing at all to take the
    average New England boy away from the Boston Herald ..."
    Nation 5 (26 December 1867): 524.

Other Printings: Lee & Shepard; Charles T. Dillingham (STARRY
    FLAG SERIES) / Lothrop, Lee & Shepard (OLIVER OPTIC SERIES
    #27; STARRY FLAG SERIES) / Street & Smith (ALGER SERIES

#155; NEW MEDAL LIBRARY #405).

Variant Titles: Seek and find: or, The mystery boy. (ALGER
   SERIES).

Locations: CtY, DLC, FTS, FU, KU, MWA, MWalB, MiEM, MnU,
   MsHAu, NHD, NN, Nh, OAU, OC, PP, TxU

059.   Shamrock and thistle: or, Young America in Ireland and
   Scotland. A story of travel and adventure by William
   T. Adams.   Lee & Shepard, c1867.   YOUNG AMERICA ABROAD
   1st series v.2.

   Copyright dated October 29, 1867, granted in the District
   of Massachusetts to William T. Adams.   Copy deposited
   December 31, 1867.   Copyright #26956 dated May 17, 1895
   for renewal on October 29, 1895.   Preface dated September
   30, 1867.

Illustrations: Anonymous; engraved by Samuel S. Kilburn.

Reviews: "This volume continues the history of the academy
   ship and her crew of boys, with their trips into the
   interior as well as voyages along the coast of Ireland
   and Scotland.   The young scholar will get a truer and
   fuller conception of these other countries by reading this
   unpretentious journal of travel, than by weeks of hard
   study upon the geographies and histories." [per L&S ad].

   "The book will interest youthful readers, for whom it is
   written.   It's style is somewhat inflated and it has a
   general tone of boyish exaggeration throughout, which we
   suppose was the intention of the author, as he wrote it
   for boys.   This however, we cannot approve, for we think
   the youth of America pick up these ideas easily enough
   without having them put before them as examples...We are
   willing to forgive the author for much of his exaggeration,
   for the fairness exhibited by him in speaking of Ireland
   and her history and her many wrongs under English rule.
   It will at least give 'Young America' a more correct idea
   of that country than can be found in 'Peter Parley's'
   books, and others of the same stamp."   Catholic World 6
   (January 1868): 574.

Other Printings: Lee & Shepard; Charles T. Dillingham (YOUNG
   AMERICA ABROAD) / Lee & Shepard; Lee, Shepard & Dillingham
   (YOUNG AMERICA ABROAD) / Lothrop, Lee & Shepard (OLIVER
   OPTIC SERIES #36; YOUNG AMERICA ABROAD).

Locations: CtY, CSmH, DLC, FTS, FU, GEU, IDekN, KU, MB, MWA,
   MWalB, MiEM, MnU, MoS, MsHAu, NHD, NN, Nh, OC, PP, PPiU,
   TxU, ViU, WM

060.   Red cross: or, Young America in England and Wales. A

story of travel and adventure by William T. Adams.
Lee & Shepard, c1867. YOUNG AMERICA ABROAD 1st series
v.3.

Copyright dated December 31, 1867, granted in the District
of Massachusetts to William T. Adams. Copy deposited
December 31, 1867. Copyright #35911 dated July 10, 1895
for renewal on December 31, 1895. Preface dated November
29, 1867.

Advertised as "Ready in December [1867]." American
Literary Gazette 10 (1 November 1867): 31.

Illustrations: Granville Perkins; engraved by Samuel S.
    Kilburn.

Description: "...chronicles the doings of the Young America
    and her crew in British ports and waters, and is replete
    with thrilling adventures and descriptions of noted
    places." [L&S ad].

Other Printings: Lee & Shepard; Charles T. Dillingham (YOUNG
    AMERICA ABROAD) / Lee & Shepard; Lee, Shepard & Dillingham
    (YOUNG AMERICA ABROAD) / Lothrop, Lee & Shepard (OLIVER
    OPTIC SERIES #37; YOUNG AMERICA ABROAD).

Locations: CSmH, DLC, FTS, FU, IDekN, KU, MB, MWA, MWalB,
    MnU, MoS, MsHAu, NHD, NN, Nh, OBgU, OC, PP, PPiU, TxU,
    WM

1868

061. Freaks of fortune: or, Half round the world. Lee &
      Shepard, c1868. STARRY FLAG SERIES v.4.

Originally appeared serially in Oliver Optic's Magazine
v.3 #53-65 (4 January - 28 March 1868).

Copyright dated October 9, 1868, granted in the District
of Massachusetts to William T. Adams. Copy deposited
October 9, 1868. Copyright #30507 dated May 19, 1896 for
renewal on October 9, 1896. Preface dated July 27, 1868.

Illustrations: W.L. Champney; engraved by Samuel S. Kilburn.

Description: "The adventures of Levi Fairfield, the noble
    young Captain of the Starry Flag, excited such an interest
    among the young folks that the continuance of his story
    was called for, with which demand the ever ready author
    has complied, with a story equally attractive and
    interesting." [L&S ad].

Reviews: "...the hero makes a voyage in his yacht to Austral-
    ia in pursuit of a young lady in whom he was deeply
    interested." Oliver Optic's Magazine 4 (26 December

1868): 834.

Other Printings: Lee & Shepard; Charles T. Dillingham (STARRY
    FLAG SERIES) / Lothrop, Lee & Shepard (OLIVER OPTIC SERIES
    #28; STARRY FLAG SERIES) / Street & Smith (ALGER SERIES
    #156; NEW MEDAL LIBRARY #412).

Variant Titles: Freaks of fortune: or, Saved from himself.
    (ALGER SERIES).

Locations: CtY, DLC, FTS, FU, KU, MB, MWA, MWalB, MiEM, MsHAu,
    NHD, NN, OAU, OC, PP, TxU, ViU

062. Make or break: or, The rich man's daughter. Lee &
        Shepard, c1868. STARRY FLAG SERIES v.5.

    Originally appeared serially in Oliver Optic's Magazine
    v.3 #66-78 (4 April - 27 June 1868).

    Copyright dated October 9, 1868, granted in the District
    of Massachusetts to William T. Adams. Copy deposited
    October 9, 1868. Copyright #30508 dated May 19, 1896,
    for renewal on October 9, 1896. Preface dated July 28,
    1868.

Illustrations: Hammatt Billings; engraved by Samuel S.
    Kilburn.

Reviews: "This is a lively, stirring volume, full of interest
    and instruction from one cover to the other. Just the
    book a smart, wide-awake boy will enjoy intensely."
    Notices of the Press. [per L&S ad].

    "...the story of a boy and girl in the humble walks of
    society, who, by living well and being true to duty, went
    'up higher.'" Oliver Optic's Magazine 4 (26 December
    1868): 834.

Other Printings: Lee & Shepard; Lee, Shepard & Dillingham
    (STARRY FLAG SERIES) / Lothrop, Lee & Shepard (OLIVER
    OPTIC SERIES #29; STARRY FLAG SERIES) / Street & Smith
    (ALGER SERIES #157; NEW MEDAL LIBRARY #418).

Variant Titles: Make or break: or, The way to succeed.
    (ALGER SERIES).

Locations: CtY, DLC, FTS, FU, MB, MWA, MiEM, MnU, MoS, MsHAu,
    NHD, NN, Nh, OAU, OC, PP, PPiU

063. Dikes and ditches: or, Young America in Holland and
        Belgium. A story of travel and adventure by William T.
        Adams. Lee & Shepard, c1868. YOUNG AMERICA ABROAD
        1st series v.4.

Copyright dated May 11, 1868, granted in the District of
Massachusetts. Copy deposited August 25, 1868. Copyright
#21523 dated April 6, 1896, for renewal on May 11, 1896.
Preface dated April 9, 1868.

Description: "The author takes his readers on voyages up the
rivers and canals of Holland and Belgium, on tramps
through the cities, their schools, their art galleries,
and their wonderful buildings, giving at every turn vivid
impressions of what is seen and heard therein and there-
abouts." [L&S ad].

Illustrations: Thomas Nast; engraved by Samuel S. Kilburn.

Reviews: "...the author takes his young readers to the lands
which Motley's histories have invested with transcendent
interest; and while he dwells at considerable length upon
the present geographical and social aspects of the country,
he cannot refrain from sketching the salient features of
that grand historic period which the historian has immor-
talized. It is to be hoped that one of the good effects
of this work will be to excite thousands of youthful minds
to read those grand historical works..." Hours at Home 7
(September 1868): 479.

Other Printings: Lee & Shepard; Lee, Shepard & Dillingham
(YOUNG AMERICA ABROAD) / Lothrop, Lee & Shepard (OLIVER
OPTIC SERIES #38; YOUNG AMERICA ABROAD).

References: Hamilton. Early American book illustrators,
#1135.

Locations: CtY, CSmH, DLC, FTS, FU, IDekN, MB, MWA, MWalB,
MnU, NHD, NN, Nh, OC, PP, PPiU, TxU, ViU, WM

064.   Down the river: or, Buck Bradford and his tyrants.
Lee & Shepard, c1868. STARRY FLAG SERIES v.6.

Originally appeared serially in Oliver Optic's Magazine
v.4 #79-91 (4 July - 26 September 1868).

Copyright dated December 3, 1868, granted in the District
of Massachusetts. Copy deposited December 15, 1868.
Copyright #42268 dated July 21, 1896, for renewal on
December 3, 1896. Preface dated October 28, 1868.

Illustrations: Thomas Nast; engraved by Samuel S. Kilburn
and Robert Varley.

Reviews: "These stories are not only written in a manner well
calculated to enchain the attention of young readers, but
teach at the same time such important lessons of sobriety,
industry and cheerfulness, that we should like to see them
in the hands of every boy in the land." Galesburg Free
Press. [per L&S ad].

"...tells the history of a boy, who, disheartened by the
cruelty of his guardians, made a voyage down the Mississippi on a raft, with his deformed sister, to New Orleans,
where his brother resided." Oliver Optic's Magazine 4
(26 December 1868): 834.

Other Printings: Lee & Shepard; Lee, Shepard & Dillingham
(STARRY FLAG SERIES) / Lothrop, Lee & Shepard (OLIVER
OPTIC SERIES #30; STARRY FLAG SERIES) / Street & Smith
(ALGER SERIES #158; NEW MEDAL LIBRARY #424).

Variant Titles: Down the river: or, Afloat and afoot.
(ALGER SERIES).

References: Hamilton. Early American book illustrators,
#1134.

Locations: CtY, DLC, FTS, FU, GEU, IDekN, MB, MWA, MWalB,
MnU, NHD, NN, Nh, OAU, OC, PP, WM

065.   Our standard-bearer: or, The life of General Ulysses S.
Grant: his youth, his manhood, his campaigns, and his
eminent services in the reconstruction of the nation
his sword has redeemed: as seen and related by Captain
Bernard Galligasken, cosmopolitan and written out by
Oliver Optic. Lee & Shepard, c1868.

Copyright dated July 27, 1868, granted in the District of
Massachusetts. Copy deposited August 25, 1868. Copyright
#21521 dated April 6, 1896 for renewal on July 27, 1896.

Illustrations: Thomas Nast; engraved by Samuel S. Kilburn and
J.T. Speer.

Reviews: Putnam's Magazine ns 2 (November 1868): 633.

References: Hamilton. Early American book illustrators,
#1134; Sabin, #57216.

Other Printings: Lee & Shepard; Charles T. Dillingham /
Lothrop, Lee, & Shepard / University Microfilms
(PRESIDENTIAL ELECTION CAMPAIGN BIOGRAPHIES PE186).

Locations: CSmH, CtY, DLC, FTS, FU, IDekN, KU, MB, MWA, MnU,
MoS, NHD, NN, Nh, PP, TxU

066.   Through by daylight: or, The young engineer of the Lake
Shore Railroad. Lee & Shepard, c1869. LAKE SHORE
SERIES v.1.

Originally appeared serially in Oliver Optic's Magazine
4 #92-104 (3 October - 26 December 1868).

Copyright dated October 4, 1869, granted in the District
of Massachusetts to William T. Adams. Copy deposited
February 21, 1870. Copyright renewal #29203 granted in
1897. Preface dated July 21, 1869.

Description: "...The young engineer is doubtless a smart boy;
    but so far as his mechanical skill is concerned, several
    counterparts of him have come to the knowledge of the
    writer. If he has an 'old head,' he has a young heart,
    which he endeavors to keep pure and true. As he appears
    in this and subsequent volumes of the series, the author
    is willing to commend him as an example of the moral and
    Christian hero, who cannot lead his imitators astray; for
    he loves truth and goodness, and is willing to forgive
    and serve his enemies." [preface].

Illustrations: W.L. Champney; engraved by Samuel S. Kilburn.

Other Printings: Lee & Shepard (AMERICAN BOYS' SERIES #55) /
    Lee & Shepard; Charles T. Dillingham (LAKE SHORE SERIES)
    / Lee & Shepard; Lee, Shepard & Dillingham (LAKE SHORE
    SERIES) / Lothrop, Lee & Shepard (AMERICAN BOYS' SERIES
    #55; LAKE SHORE SERIES; OLIVER OPTIC SERIES #13) /
    Street & Smith (ALGER SERIES #147; NEW MEDAL LIBRARY #430).

Variant Titles: Through by daylight: or, King of the rails.
    (ALGER SERIES).

Locations: CSmH, DLC, FTS, FU, IDekN, MB, MWA, MWalB, MnU,
    MsHAu, NHD, NN, Nh, OAU, OC, PP, ViU, WM

067. Palace and cottage: or, Young America in France and
        Switzerland. A story of travel and adventure by
        William T. Adams. Lee & Shepard, c1868. YOUNG
        AMERICA ABROAD 1st series v.5.

    Copyright dated December 22, 1868, granted in the District
    of Massachusetts to William T. Adams. Copy deposited Jan-
    uary 21, 1869. Copyright #42269 dated December 21, 1896
    for renewal on December 22, 1896. Preface dated November
    23, 1868.

Description: " ...relates the history of the American Squad-
    ron (Young America and Josephine) in the waters of France,
    with the journey of the students to Paris and through a
    portion of Switzerland. As an episode, the story of the
    runaway cruise of the Josephine is introduced, inculcating
    the moral that 'the way of the transgressor is hard.'"
    [L&S ad].

Illustrations: Granville Perkins and George G. White;
    engraved by John Andrew.

Reviews: "...It follows the history of the students of the
    Academy Ship and her consort into the waters of France,

...and through Switzerland. It has also the story of
certain runaways, who, under an organization called
'The Knights of the Golden Fleece,' captured the consort
of the ship, and attempted to make a voyage in her. The
book contains a sketch of the countries visited, a state-
ment of their physical features, forms of government, and
the manners and customs of the people." Oliver Optic's
Magazine 4 (26 December 1868): 834.

Other Printings: Lee & Shepard; Lee, Shepard & Dillingham
    (YOUNG AMERICA ABROAD) / Lothrop, Lee & Shepard (OLIVER
    OPTIC SERIES #39; YOUNG AMERICA ABROAD).

Locations: CtY, CSmH, DLC, FU, IDekN, MB, MWA, MWalB, MnU,
    MoS, MsHAu, NHD, NN, Nh, OBgU, OC, PP, PPiU, TxU, ViU, WM

                    1869

068.   Lightning Express: or, The rival academies.   Lee &
       Shepard, c1869. LAKE SHORE SERIES v.2.

    Originally appeared serially in Oliver Optic's Magazine
    5 #105-117 (2 January - 27 March 1869).

    Copyright dated October 4, 1869, granted in the District
    of Massachusetts to William T. Adams. Copy deposited
    February 21, 1870. Copyright renewal #29204 granted in
    1897 to Alice Adams Russell. Two copies deposited at LC
    on November 12, 1897. Preface dated July 21, 1869.

Description: "...The story, like its predecessor, relates to
    the Lake Shore Railroad...The author...is not afraid that
    any reasonable young man will like either Tommy [Topple-
    ton] or Waddie [Wimpleton] well enough to imitate their
    conduct, while he is satisfied that all will be pleased
    with the moral heroism of Wolf Penniman, and will indorse
    his views of Christian duty." [preface].

Illustrations: Reimunt Sayer; engraved by Samuel S. Kilburn.

Other Printings: Lee & Shepard; Charles T. Dillingham (LAKE
    SHORE SERIES) / Lee & Shepard; Lee, Shepard & Dillingham
    (LAKE SHORE SERIES) / Lothrop, Lee & Shepard (LAKE SHORE
    SERIES; OLIVER OPTIC SERIES #14) / Street & Smith (ALGER
    SERIES #148; NEW MEDAL LIBRARY #435).

Variant Titles: Lightning Express: or, Sure hand and keen
    eye. (ALGER SERIES).

References: Hamilton. Early American book illustrators,
    #1196.

Locations: CSmH, DLC, FTS, FU, GEU, IDekN, MB, MWA, MWalB,
    MiEM, MnU, MsHAu, NHD, NN, Nh, OC, PP, ViU, WM

069. On time: or, The young captain of the Ucayga steamer.
      Lee & Shepard, c1869. LAKE SHORE SERIES v.3.

      Originally appeared serially in Oliver Optic's Magazine
      v.5 #118-130 (3 April - 26 June 1869).

      Copyright dated October 4, 1869, granted in the District
      of Massachusetts to William T. Adams. Copy deposited
      February 21, 1870. Copyright renewal #29205 granted in
      1897 to Alice Adams Russell. Preface dated July 21, 1869.

Description: "...The writer has endeavored, in these pages,
      to illustrate the blessed precept, 'Love your enemies,'
      and to convince his young friends that a wide-awake boy
      may have the principles of the gospel in his heart, and
      may carry them into practice in his daily life."
      [preface].

Illustrations: John J. Harley; engraved by Samuel S. Kilburn.

Other Printings: Lee & Shepard; Charles T. Dillingham (LAKE
      SHORE SERIES) / Lothrop, Lee & Shepard (LAKE SHORE SERIES;
      OLIVER OPTIC SERIES #15) / Street & Smith (ALGER SERIES
      #149; NEW MEDAL LIBRARY #441).

Variant Titles: On time: or, Bound to get there. (ALGER
      SERIES).

Locations: CSmH, DLC, FTS, FU, GEU, IDekN, KU, MB, MWA, MWalB,
      MiEM, MnU, MsHAu, NHD, NN, Nh, OC, PP, TxU, ViU, WM

070. Switch off: or, The war of the students. Lee & Shepard,
      c1869. LAKE SHORE SERIES v.4.

      Originally appeared serially in Oliver Optic's Magazine
      v.6 #131-143 (3 July - 25 September 1869).

      Copyright dated October 4, 1869, granted in the District
      of Massachusetts to William T. Adams. Copy deposited
      February 21, 1870. Copyright renewal #29206 granted in
      1897 to Alice Adams Russell. Preface dated August 24,
      1869.

Description: "...Its principal incidents relate to the
      students of the Toppleton Institute, among whom the war
      indicated on the title-page occurred...Tommy Toppleton
      again appears, and is even more overbearing and tyran-
      nical than before; but the reader will be willing to
      congratulate him, at the end,...The manner in which peace
      happened to be made between the rival Institutes has al-
      ways been found to work quite as well in actual experience
      as in the story." [preface].

Illustrations: Henry W. Herrick; engraved by Samuel S. Kil-
      burn.

Other Printings: Lee & Shepard; Charles T. Dillingham (LAKE
    SHORE SERIES) / Lothrop, Lee & Shepard (LAKE SHORE SERIES;
    OLIVER OPTIC SERIES #16) / Street & Smith (ALGER SERIES
    #150; NEW MEDAL LIBRARY #447).

Variant Titles: Switch off: or, When danger threatens.
    (ALGER SERIES).

References: Hamilton. Early American book illustrators, #837.

Locations: CSmH, CtY, DLC, FTS, FU, IDekN, KU, MB, MWA, MWalB,
    MiEM, MnU, MoS, MsHAu, NHD, NN, Nh, OC, PP, TxU, ViU, WM

071. Brake up: or, The young peacemakers. Lee & Shepard,
       c1870. LAKE SHORE SERIES v.5.

    Originally appeared serially in Oliver Optic's Magazine
    v.6 #144-156 (2 October - 25 December 1869).

    Copyright dated February 18, 1870, granted in the District
    of Massachusetts to William T. Adams. Copy deposited Feb-
    ruary 21, 1870. Copyright renewal #4169 dated February
    18, 1898. Preface dated January 26, 1870.

Description: "...While Captain Wolf Penniman still remains
    true to his high standard of duty, Nick Van Wolter is
    presented to the reader in strong contrast with the hero
    ...The railroad phrase 'Brake Up' is not used in its
    technical sense, but figuratively indicates how the wrong-
    doer should proceed when he becomes conscious of his
    error..." [preface].

Illustrations: John J. Harley; engraved by Samuel S. Kilburn.

Other Printings: Lee & Shepard; Lee, Shepard & Dillingham
    (LAKE SHORE SERIES) / Lothrop, Lee & Shepard (LAKE SHORE
    SERIES; OLIVER OPTIC SERIES #17) / Street & Smith (ALGER
    SERIES #151; NEW MEDAL LIBRARY #453).

Variant Titles: Brake up: or, A roving commission. (ALGER
    SERIES).

Locations: CSmH, CtY, DLC, FTS, FU, GEU, IDekN, MB, MWA,
    MWalB, MiEM, MnU, MsHAu, NHD, NN, Nh, OC, PP, TxU, WM

072. Down the Rhine: or, Young America in Germany. A story
       of travel and adventure by William T. Adams. Lee &
       Shepard, c1869. YOUNG AMERICA ABROAD 1st series v.6.

    Copyright dated November 1, 1869, granted in the District
    of Massachusetts to William T. Adams. Copy deposited
    November 19, 1869. Copyright renewal #29207 dated 1897.
    Preface dated October 28, 1869.

Illustrations: Anonymous; engraved by John Andrew.

Reviews: "This volume concludes the first series of Young
    America, and is as interesting and instructive as the
    preceding volumes. So great has been the success of
    this series, that Oliver Optic is now preparing a
    second..." [per L&S ad].

    "Several delightful books for the young folks remain to
    be noticed. They are another volume of Oliver Optic's
    popular series, Young America Abroad, the present being
    entitled Down the Rhine..." Hours at Home 10 (February
    1870): 388.

Other Printings: Lee & Shepard; Lee, Shepard & Dillingham
    (YOUNG AMERICA ABROAD) / Lothrop, Lee & Shepard (OLIVER
    OPTIC SERIES #40; YOUNG AMERICA ABROAD).

Locations: CtY, CSmH, DLC, FTS, FU, IDekN, KU, MB, MWA, MWalB,
    MiEM, MnU, MoS, MsHAu, NHD, NN, Nh, OBgU, OC, PP, PPiU,
    TxU, ViU, WM

                          1870

073.   Standard historical stories [including The soldier boy,
       The young lieutenant, and Fighting Joe]; embellished
       with an allegorical presentation page and ten full
       page illustrations from the pencils of Nast, Champney,
       and other well known artists. Richardson, c1870.
       People's edition.

Copyright #2504 dated October 5, 1870.

Illustrations: Thomas Nast, W.L. Champney, and others.

Locations: DLC, MWA

074.   Bear and forbear: or, The young skipper of Lake Ucayga.
       Lee & Shepard, c1870. LAKE SHORE SERIES v.6.

    Originally appeared serially in Oliver Optic's Magazine
    v.7 #157-169 (1 January - 26 March 1870).

    Copyright #309 dated July 27, 1870 granted to William T.
    Adams. Two copies deposited at LC on August 20, 1870.
    Copyright renewal #10970 dated 1898 granted to Alice Adams
    Russell. Two copies deposited at LC on September 8, 1898.
    Preface dated June 1, 1870.

    Advertised as "This day published." American Literary
    Gazette 15 (1 September 1870).

Illustrations: Reimunt Sayer; engraved by Samuel S. Kilburn.

Description: "...The characters that have been prominent in
    the other volumes...are again presented, to be finally
    dealt with according to their several deserts. The writer
    has endeavored to show that fidelity to duty prospers even
    in this world, and that evil doing brings pain and misery;
    and if he has awarded 'poetical justice' to each, it will
    only make the contrast the more evident..." [preface].

Reviews: "Oliver Optic's books are always great favorites
    with the young people. This is quite as interesting as
    the rest of the series." Catholic World 12 (December
    1870): 431.

    Also reviewed in Harper's Magazine 42 (January 1871):
    304; Old and New 2 (December 1870): 739.

Other Printings: Lee & Shepard; Lee, Shepard & Dillingham
    (LAKE SHORE SERIES) / Lothrop, Lee & Shepard (LAKE SHORE
    SERIES; OLIVER OPTIC SERIES #18) / Street & Smith (ALGER
    SERIES #152; NEW MEDAL LIBRARY #460).

Variant Titles: Bear and forbear: or, On his mettle. (ALGER
    SERIES).

Locations: CSmH, DLC, FTS, FU, IDekN, KU, MB, MWA, MWalB,
    MiEM, MnU, MoS, MsHAu, NHD, NN, Nh, OC, PP, TxU, ViU, WM

075.   Field and forest: or, The fortunes of a farmer. Lee &
    Shepard, c1870. UPWARD AND ONWARD SERIES v.1.

    Originally appeared serially in Oliver Optic's Magazine
    7 #170-182 (2 April - 25 June 1870).

    Copyright #2643 dated October 8, 1870, granted to William
    T. Adams. Two copies deposited at LC on October 29, 1870.
    Preface dated June 6, 1870.

Illustrations: Henry W. Herrick; engraved by Samuel S. Kil-
    burn.

Reviews: "Oliver Optic's books are too well known to need
    commendation: they have been the favorite books of boys
    for years past. The Upward and Onward series promises
    to be quite as attractive as any of the others; but his
    reign over boy-literature seems about to be seriously
    disputed." Catholic World 12 (March 1871): 859-60.

    Also reviewed in Old and New 3 (January 1871): 109; Our
    Young Folks 7 (January 1871): 63.

Other Printings: Lee & Shepard (AMERICAN BOYS' SERIES #51) /
    Lee & Shepard; Charles T. Dillingham (UPWARD AND ONWARD
    SERIES) / Lee & Shepard; Lee, Shepard & Dillingham
    (UPWARD AND ONWARD SERIES) / Lothrop, Lee & Shepard
    (AMERICAN BOYS' SERIES #51; OLIVER OPTIC SERIES #48;

UPWARD AND ONWARD SERIES).

Locations: CSmH, DLC, FTS, FU, MB, MWA, MWalB, MiEM, MnU,
 MsHAu, NHD, Nh, OC, PP, WM

076. <u>Plane and plank: or, The mishaps of a mechanic.</u> Lee &
 Shepard, c1870. UPWARD AND ONWARD SERIES v.2.

Originally appeared serially in <u>Oliver Optic's Magazine</u>
8 #183-195 (2 July - 24 September 1870).

Copyright #3859 dated November 18, 1870, granted to
William T. Adams. Two copies deposited at LC on November
21, 1870. Copyright renewal #37369 issued in 1898.
Preface dated June 7, 1870.

Illustrations: Henry W. Herrick; engraved by Samuel S. Kilburn.

Reviews: See <u>Field and forest</u> (75) for review.

Other Printings: Lee & Shepard; Charles T. Dillingham
 (UPWARD AND ONWARD SERIES) / Lee & Shepard; Lee,
 Shepard & Dillingham (UPWARD AND ONWARD SERIES) /
 Lothrop, Lee & Shepard (UPWARD AND ONWARD SERIES).

Locations: CSmH, CtY, DLC, FTS, FU, MB, MWA, MWalB, MnU,
 MoS, MsHAu, NHD, NN, Nh, OAU, OC, PP, TxU, ViU, WM

077. <u>Desk and debit: or, The catastrophes of a clerk.</u> Lee &
 Shepard, c1871. UPWARD AND ONWARD SERIES v.3.

Originally appeared serially in <u>Oliver Optic's Magazine</u>
8 #196-209 (1 October - 31 December 1870).

Copyright #2316 dated March 18, 1871, granted to William
T. Adams. Two copies deposited at LC on April 21, 1871.
Copyright renewal #5427 issued in 1899. Preface dated
June 7, 1870.

Illustrations: Henry W. Herrick; engraved by Samuel S. Kilburn.

Reviews: "This is one of the new 'Upward and Onward' series,
 and the tale is written in that peculiarly happy style
 which has made Oliver Optic's name so familiar to all
 boys and girls." <u>American Literary Gazette</u> 17 (15 May
 1871): 39.

Other Printings: Lee & Shepard; Charles T. Dillingham
 (UPWARD & ONWARD SERIES) / Lee & Shepard; Lee, Shepard &
 Dillingham (UPWARD AND ONWARD SERIES) / Lothrop, Lee &
 Shepard (UPWARD AND ONWARD SERIES).

References: Hamilton. Early American book illustrators, #838.

Locations: CtY, DLC, FTS, FU, KU, MB, MWA, MWalB, MnU,
    MsHAu, NHD, NN, Nh, OC, PP, ViU, WM

1871

078. Oliver Optic's almanac for our boys and girls...1872.
      Containing calendars for the months, memorandum
      diary for everyday in the year. Lee & Shepard, 1871.

    Advertised in American Literary Gazette 18 (December
    1871, Christmas Supplement).

Reviews: Oliver Optic's Magazine 11 (January 1872): 79.

Locations: DLC, OC

079. Cringle and cross-tree: or, The sea swashes of a sailor.
      Lee & Shepard, c1871. UPWARD AND ONWARD SERIES v.4.

    Originally appeared serially in Oliver Optic's Magazine
    9 #210-215 (January - June 1871).

    Copyright #8667 dated September 16, 1871, granted to
    William T. Adams. Two copies deposited at LC on February
    26, 1872. Copyright renewal #42673 issued in 1899.
    Preface dated August 21, 1871.

Illustrations: Henry L. Stephens; engraved by John Andrew.

Reviews: "Oliver Optic's store of tales for boys seems to be
    inexhaustible. Precocious development of 'muscular
    Christianity' is a particularly pleasing theme with boys,
    and, as it enters largely into this story, the book will
    be proportionately popular." American Literary Gazette
    17 (16 October 1871): 363.

Other Printings: Lee & Shepard; Charles T. Dillingham (UPWARD
    AND ONWARD SERIES) / Lee & Shepard; Lee, Shepard & Dill-
    ingham (UPWARD AND ONWARD SERIES) / Lothrop, Lee & Shepard
    (UPWARD AND ONWARD SERIES).

Locations: DLC, FTS, FU, GEU, MB, MWA, MWalB, MnU, MsHAu, NHD,
    NN, Nh, OC, PP, ViU

080. Up the Baltic: or, Young America in Norway, Sweden, and
      Denmark. A story of travel and adventure by William
      T. Adams. Lee & Shepard, c1871. YOUNG AMERICA ABROAD
      2nd series v.1.

    Copyright #5121 dated May 31, 1871, granted to William T.
    Adams. Two copies deposited at LC on June 16, 1871.

Copyright renewal #18655 dated 1899. Preface dated May 10, 1871.

Description: "A record of what was seen and done by the young gentlemen of the Academy Squadron on its second voyage to Europe, embracing its stay in the waters of Norway, Sweden, and Denmark." [preface].

Illustrations: Anonymous; engraved by John Andrew.

Reviews: "This is one of those tales, full of adventures, by which Oliver Optic's name has become a household word with boys. We are not quite sure, however, that some of the doings of the youthful heroes are examples of the right sort for boys to follow. The love of mischief is inherent in most boys, and does not require the prompting a tale of this kind offers. However, it has a thoroughly healthy moral tone, and if it errs on the side of mischief, boys are not likely to read it less on that account. The illustrations are plentiful, and well executed." American Literary Gazette 17 (1 July 1871): 122.

Also reviewed in Literary World 2 (1 July 1871): 29.

Other Printings: Lee & Shepard; Lee, Shepard & Dillingham (YOUNG AMERICA ABROAD) / Lothrop, Lee & Shepard (AMERICAN BOYS' SERIES #100; OLIVER OPTIC SERIES #41; YOUNG AMERICA ABROAD).

Locations: CtY, CSmH, DLC, FTS, FU, GEU, IDekN, MB, MWA, MWalB, MnU, MsHAu, NHD, NN, Nh, OAU, OBgU, OC, PP, PPiU, TxU, ViU

081. Bivouac and battle: or, The struggles of a soldier.
      Lee & Shepard, c1871. UPWARD AND ONWARD SERIES v.5.

Originally appeared serially in Oliver Optic's Magazine 10 #216-221 (July - December 1871).

Copyright #11966 dated December 18, 1871, granted to William T. Adams. Copyright renewal #67490 dated October 18, 1899. Preface dated November 25, 1871.

Illustrations: Henry L. Stephens.

Reviews: "The two young heroes of this story serve through the Italian campaign in company with the French Army in 1859. They meet with many strange adventures, and more than once their youthful careers are in danger of an abrupt termination; but fortune befriends them, and the object of their visit to Italy is safely accomplished." American Literary Gazette 18 (15 January 1872): 99.

"Two juveniles by favorite authors, are issued just in time to catch the holiday breeze of demand...Bivouac and

Battle..." Literary World 2 (1 January 1872): 124.

Also reviewed in Youth's Companion 45 (25 January 1872): 31.

Other Printings: Lee & Shepard; Charles T. Dillingham (UPWARD AND ONWARD SERIES) / Lee & Shepard; Lee, Shepard & Dillingham (UPWARD AND ONWARD SERIES) / Lothrop, Lee & Shepard (UPWARD AND ONWARD SERIES).

Locations: DLC, FTS, FU, GEU, IDekN, MB, MWA, NHD, NN, MnU, MsHAu, Nh, OC, PP, ViU, WM

1872

082. Sea and shore: or, The tramps of a traveller. Lee & Shepard, c1872. UPWARD AND ONWARD SERIES v.6.

Originally appeared serially in Oliver Optic's Magazine v.11 #222-227 (January - June 1872).

Copyright #5337 dated May 22, 1872, granted to William T. Adams. Two copies deposited at LC on June 11, 1872. Copyright renewal #A5069 granted to Alice Adams Russell in 1900. Preface dated April 20, 1870.

Illustrations: Granville Perkins; engraved by John Andrew.

Reviews: "...It exhibits Phil Farringford, the hero, as captain of a gallant yacht, and describes an exciting chase, in which his vessel is the pursuer." Literary World 3 (1 July 1872): 27.

Other Printings: Lee & Shepard; Charles T. Dillingham (UPWARD AND ONWARD SERIES) / Lee & Shepard; Lee, Shepard & Dillingham (UPWARD AND ONWARD SERIES) / Lothrop, Lee & Shepard (UPWARD AND ONWARD SERIES).

Locations: CtY, DLC, FTS, FU, GEU, MB, MWA, MnU, MsHAu, NHD, NN, OAU, OC, PP, ViU

083. Northern lands: or, Young America in Russia and Prussia. A story of travel and adventure by William T. Adams. Lee & Shepard, c1872. YOUNG AMERICA ABROAD 2nd series v.2.

Copyright #1774 dated February 23, 1872, granted to William T. Adams. Copyright renewal #310 dated January 3, 1900. Preface dated December 18, 1871.

Description: "...describes the varied experience of the juvenile tourists of the Academy Squadron in the Baltic, and during their journeys in Russia and Prussia, and their voyages between the different ports in these countries..." [preface].

Illustrations: Granville Perkins.

Reviews: "The second volume of the second series of Oliver
    Optic's 'Young America Abroad' stories is entitled
    'Northern Lands' and introduces the reader to Russia
    and Prussia, which he sees in the agreeable company of
    the young gentlemen who man the Academy Squadron..."
    Literary World 2 (1 April 1872): 171.

Other Printings: Lee & Shepard; Lee, Shepard & Dillingham
    (YOUNG AMERICA ABROAD) / Lothrop, Lee & Shepard (OLIVER
    OPTIC SERIES #42; YOUNG AMERICA ABROAD).

Locations: CtY, CSmH, DLC, FTS, FU, GEU, IDekN, MB, MWA,
    MWalB, MnU, MoS, MsHAu, NHD, NN, Nh, OAU, OBgU, OC, PP,
    PPiU, TxU, ViU

084.   Little Bobtail: or, The wreck of the Penobscot.   Lee &
        Shepard, c1872.   YACHT CLUB SERIES v.1.

    Originally appeared serially in Oliver Optic's Magazine
    v.12 #228-233 (July - December 1872).

    Copyright #12553 dated November 29, 1872, granted to
    William T. Adams. Two copies deposited at LC on December
    7, 1872. Copyright renewal #A15884 dated June 17, 1900.
    Two copies deposited at LC on June 23, 1909. Preface
    dated October 10, 1872.

Illustrations: Charles G. Bush; engraved by John Andrew.

Reviews: "Little Bobtail is one of Oliver Optic's best
    stories. The hero, the son of a very wealthy man, has
    been reared in obscurity, but finally is recognized by
    his father and restored to his rightful position. The
    book is mainly occupied by an account of his boyish
    adventures on the water. The scene of the story is laid
    at Camden, Maine." Literary World 3 (1 March 1873): 155.

Other Printings: Lee & Shepard; Lee, Shepard & Dillingham
    (YACHT CLUB SERIES) / Lothrop, Lee & Shepard (AMERICAN
    BOYS' SERIES #90; OLIVER OPTIC SERIES #49; YACHT CLUB
    SERIES).

Locations: CSmH, DLC, FTS, FU, GEU, IDekN, MB, MWA, MWalB,
    MnU, MsHAu, NHD, NN, Nh, PP, TxU, ViU, WM

085.   Cross and crescent: or, Young America in Turkey and
        Greece. A story of travel and adventure by William T.
        Adams. Lee & Shepard, c1872.   YOUNG AMERICA ABROAD
        2nd series v.3.

Copyright #12913 dated December 9, 1872, granted to William T. Adams. Two copies deposited at LC on December 27,
1872. Copyright renewal #A19996 dated August 11, 1900,
granted to Alice Adams Russell. Two copies deposited at
LC on June 23, 1909. Preface dated November 18, 1872.

Illustrations: Anonymous; engraved by John Andrew.

Reviews: "This is the third volume of the second series of
Young America Abroad and like all the rest of the series,
is most instructive and entertaining." Catholic World 16
(March 1873): 859.

"...exhibits the Academy Squadron in the waters of Turkey
and Greece. It supplies a good deal of information about
these countries in an agreeable form, and in combination
with a readable story in which the young men of the
squadron are the chief actors. We think the author errs
in giving so much space to the illustration of mean
'streaks' in the natures of some of the boys." Literary
World 3 (1 March 1873): 155.

Also reviewed in Independent 25 (20 March 1873): 363.

Other Printings: Lee & Shepard; Lee, Shepard & Dillingham
(YOUNG AMERICA ABROAD) / Lothrop, Lee & Shepard (OLIVER
OPTIC SERIES #43; YOUNG AMERICA ABROAD).

Locations: CSmH, DLC, FU, IDekN, KU, MB, MWA, MWalB, MiEM,
MnU, MoS, MsHAu, NHD, NN, Nh, OAU, OC, PP, PPiU, TxU, ViU

1873

086. In school and college: a tale for youth [by William
Taylor Adams]. Pott, Young, 1873.

Adams is the supposed author of this work. Authorship
attributed to Adams by bookseller. Item in Columbia
University Library holdings.

087. The yacht club: or, The young boat-builder. Lee &
Shepard, c1873. YACHT CLUB SERIES v.2.

Originally appeared serially in Oliver Optic's Magazine
v.13 #234-239 (January - June 1873).

Copyright #11034 dated September 25, 1873, granted to
William T. Adams. Two copies deposited at LC on October
11, 1873. Copyright renewal #A16962. Preface dated May
22, 1873.

Description: "The interest centers in Don John, the Boat-
builder, who is certainly a very enterprising young man,
though his achievements have been more than paralleled

in the domain of actual life...The most important lesson
in morals to be derived from his experience is that it
is unwise and dangerous for young people to conceal
their actions from their parents and friends..."
[preface].

Illustrations: Charles G. Bush; engraved by John Andrew.

Reviews: "Though some of the characters of the first volume
of the series 'Little Bobtail,' appear in this, it is not
a continuation of that very interesting juvenile. Like
the latter story, most of the incidents occur on the
waters of Penobscot Bay, where several yacht races take
place, which are described in a way to win the hearts of
all interested in this exciting sport...contains thirteen
very good illustrations." Publishers Weekly 4 (4 October
1873): 350.

Other Printings: Lee & Shepard; Lee, Shepard & Dillingham
(YACHT CLUB SERIES) / Lothrop, Lee & Shepard (YACHT CLUB
SERIES).

Locations: CtY, CSmH, DLC, FTS, FU, MB, MWA, MWalB, MnU,
MsHAu, NHD, NN, Nh, OBgU, OC, PP, TxU, ViU

088.   "A brave boy's fortune."

Copyright #1648 dated February 18, 1873, granted to
George Munro. Two copies deposited at LC on February
18, 1873.

Appeared serially in New York Fireside Companion 17
March - 30 June 1873.

This title has not been located in book form.

089.   Money-maker: or, The victory of the Basilisk. Lee &
       Shepard, c1873. YACHT CLUB SERIES v.3.

Originally appeared serially in Oliver Optic's Magazine
v.14 #240-245 (July - December 1873).

Copyright #13724 dated November 26, 1873, granted to
William T. Adams. Two copies deposited at LC on Dec. 27,
1873. Preface dated October 15, 1873.

Description: "...Morris Hollinghead, the hero, certainly
is not a baby, and the author does not believe he is a
'prig'..." [preface].

Illustrations: Charles G. Bush; engraved by John Andrew.

Reviews: "...the hero is a member of the 'Yacht Club,' and
many of the most exciting events are the regattas of the

club, in which several of the young boatmen who figure
in the preceding books take an active part, the main
events of the narrative form a distinct story. We think
the boys will like it even better than the rest of the
series. It is nicely gotten up and contains thirteen
illustrations." Publishers Weekly 4 (13 December 1873):
668-9.

Other Printings: Lee & Shepard; Lee, Shepard & Dillingham
    (YACHT CLUB SERIES) / Lothrop, Lee & Shepard (YACHT CLUB
    SERIES).

Locations: CtY, CSmH, DLC, FTS, FU, IDekN, MB, MWA, MWalB,
    MnU, MsHAu, NHD, NN, Nh, OC, PP, TxU, ViU, WM

090. "True to his aim. A story for old and young."

    Copyright #11205 dated October 1, 1873, granted to Lee &
    Shepard. No record of copies deposited.

    This title has not been located in book format. There
    is a possibility that this title was never published.

                          1874

091. The coming wave: or, The hidden treasure of High Rock.
        Lee & Shepard, c1874. YACHT CLUB SERIES v.4.

    Originally appeared serially in Oliver Optic's Magazine
    v.15 #246-251 (January - June 1874).

    Copyright #10960 dated August 22, 1874, granted to William
    T. Adams. Two copies deposited at LC on October 16, 1874.
    Copyright renewal #A11546. Preface dated July 10, 1874.

Description: "Leopold Bennington and Stumpy are the chief
    characters. They are both working boys...They are fastid-
    iously honest, and strictly upright, though they make
    mistakes like other human beings..." [preface].

Illustrations: Anonymous; engraved by John Andrew.

Other Printings: Lee & Shepard; Lee, Shepard & Dillingham
    (YACHT CLUB SERIES) / Lothrop, Lee & Shepard (YACHT
    CLUB SERIES).

Locations: CSmH, DLC, FTS, FU, IDekN, MB, MWA, MWalB, MiEM,
    MnU, MsHAu, NHD, NN, OC, PP, ViU, WM

092. The Dorcas Club: or, Our girls afloat. Lee & Shepard,
        c1874. YACHT CLUB SERIES v.5.

Originally appeared serially in Oliver Optic's Magazine
v.16 #252-257 (July - December 1874).

Copyright #14505 dated December 2, 1874, granted to William T. Adams. Two copies deposited at LC on December 7,
1874. Copyright renewal #A37382. Preface dated October
21, 1874.

Illustrations: Lewis J. Bridgman; engraved by John Andrew.

Reviews: "...story of some young girls who organized a boat-
    club, but spent more time in deliberation and debate than
    in nautical exercise. The hero of the book is a fine young
    fellow, who is the ward of a miserly and dishonest uncle,
    and the narrative of his resistance to his relative's evil
    schemes is quite interesting." Literary World 5 (January
    1875): 124.

"A party of young girls, who have formed themselves into a
    'Dorcas Society' for the relief of the poor, conceive the
    idea of buying a boat and learning to row it, for the sake
    of pleasure and exercise. The success attending their
    plan, and their various adventures, form the chief portion
    of the story, although there is a hero, persecuted by a
    rich and miserly guardian, who turns out the villain of the
    story." Publishers Weekly 6 (19 December 1874): 677.

Also reviewed in Saturday Review 39 (March 1875): 425, 427.

Other Printings: Lee & Shepard; Charles T. Dillingham (YACHT
    CLUB) / Lee & Shepard; Lee, Shepard & Dillingham (YACHT
    CLUB SERIES) / Lothrop, Lee & Shepard (YACHT CLUB SERIES).

Locations: CtY, CSmH, DLC, FTS, FU, IDekN, MB, MWA, MiEM, MnU,
    MsHAu, NHD, NN, Nh, PP, ViU

093. Sunny shores: or, Young America in Italy and Austria.
      A story of travel and adventure by William T. Adams.
      Lee & Shepard, c1874. YOUNG AMERICA ABROAD 2nd series
      v.4.

Copyright #12796 dated October 15, 1874, granted to William
T. Adams. Two copies deposited at LC on October 16, 1874.
Preface dated August 24, 1874.

Illustrations: Anonymous; engraved by John Andrew.

Reviews: "...In it are narrated the adventures of the Academy
    boys in Italy and Austria, a good deal of useful informa-
    tion about these countries being mingled with interesting
    incidents of the voyage." Literary World 5 (November 1874):
    92.

Also reviewed in Publishers Weekly Christmas Supplement
(December 1873): 14.

Other Printings: Lee & Shepard; Lee, Shepard & Dillingham
    (YOUNG AMERICA ABROAD) / Lothrop, Lee & Shepard (OLIVER
    OPTIC SERIES #44; YOUNG AMERICA ABROAD).

Locations: CtY, CSmH, DLC, FTS, FU, GEU, IDekN, MB, MWA,
    MWalB, MiEM, MnU, MoE, MsHAu, NHD, NN, Nh, OAU, OBgU, OC,
    PP, TxU, ViU

                            1875

094. Dedicatory hymn.

    Text of the speech delivered by Adams at the dedication
    of the Dorchester [Boston] branch library in 1875.

095. Getting an indorser, and other stories. Lee & Shepard,
        c1875.

    Copyright granted to William T. Adams in 1875.

    Contents: Getting an indorser -- Six hundred a year --
    The new minister: or, 'Charity begins at home' -- 'Out
    nights': or, Belonging to the 'Sons' -- Send for the
    doctor -- The mercantile angel -- The bachelor beau.

    Some of the same stories also appeared in Marrying
    a beggar (12) and In doors and out (2).

    Reprinted in part from various periodicals.

Other Printings: Lee & Shepard (HEARTHSTONE SERIES v.4).

Locations: DLC, MnU, NHD, NN

096. Ocean-born: or, The cruise of the clubs. Lee & Shepard,
        c1875. YACHT CLUB SERIES v.6.

    Originally appeared serially in Oliver Optic's Magazine
    v.17 #258-263 (January - June 1875).

    Copyright #5080 dated May 12, 1875 granted, to William T.
    Adams. Two copies deposited at LC on May 20, 1875.
    Copyright renewal #A58512. Preface dated March 12, 1875.

Description: "Though the hero sails on the ocean in a steam
    yacht, he is a young man of high aims and noble purposes.
    His character is worthy of the respect and imitation of
    the reader." [Preface].

Illustrations: W.L. Sheppard; engraved by John Andrew.

Reviews: "The sixth and last volume of the 'Yacht Club
    Series,' and, like its predecessors, an independent story.

Many old friends, however, will be found in it, and the same amount of sea and land adventures as the rest of the series contain, and even of a more romantic character, if possible." Publishers Weekly 7 (5 June 1875): 597.

Other Printings: Lee & Shepard; Charles T. Dillingham (YACHT CLUB SERIES) / Lee & Shepard; Lee, Shepard & Dillingham (YACHT CLUB SERIES) / Lothrop, Lee & Shepard (YACHT CLUB SERIES).

Locations: CSmH, DLC, FTS, FU, GEU, IDekN, MB, MnU, MsHAu, NHD, NN, Nh

097. "Mending his ways."

Appeared serially in New York Fireside Companion 24 May - 20 September 1875.

This title has not been located in book form.

098. Going west: or, The perils of a poor boy. Lee & Shepard, c1875. GREAT WESTERN SERIES v.1.

Originally appeared serially in Oliver Optic's Magazine v.18 #264-269 (July - December 1875).

Copyright #12701 dated December 2, 1875, granted to William T. Adams. Two copies deposited at LC on December 9, 1875. Copyright renewal #A62391. Preface dated November 1, 1875.

Description: "[The hero] is a young sailor...at first he is not a boy of much spirit, but he soon develops this attribute...The story takes him to the Great West, where he finds a home...on one of the great lakes." [preface].

Illustrations: Anonymous.

Reviews: "'Going West' is the initial volume...It is complete in itself; but the further career of the hero, a young sailor, will be described in subsequent volumes. The author has prepared himself to write this series by extensive travels in the West; and put into it, if we may judge by this volume, a good deal of information, as well as entertainment..." Literary World 6 (January 1876): 116.

"...The hero of this story is a poor boy, who begins life in the very humblest position, and goes through many perils and temptations, finally finding a home in the great West. The chief portion of the young boy's story takes place on board ship giving a good deal of life and experience among sailors." Publishers Weekly 8 (18 December 1875): 936.

Other Printings: Lee & Shepard; Charles T. Dillingham (GREAT

WESTERN SERIES) / Lothrop, Lee & Shepard (AMERICAN BOYS'
SERIES #89; GREAT WESTERN SERIES; OLIVER OPTIC SERIES #47).

Locations: DLC, FTS, FU, MB, MWA, MWalB, MnU, MsHAu, NHD,
    OBgU, OC, PP, TxU, WM

099. The great bonanza: illustrated narrative of adventure
        and discovery in gold mining, silver mining, among the
        raftsmen, in the oil regions, whaling, hunting, fish-
        ing, and fighting. By Oliver Optic, R.M. Ballantyne,
        T.W. Higginson, C.E. Bishop, Capt. Chas. W. Hall, Frank
        H. Taylor. With 200 illustrations by W.L. Sheppard,
        Frank Merrill, H.L. Stephens, Miss L.B. Humphrey and
        other well-known artists. Lee & Shepard, c1875.

    Copyright #7942 dated July 28, 1875, granted to Lee &
    Shepard. Two copies deposited at LC on November 15, 1875.

Illustrations: Miss Lisbeth B. Humphrey, Frank Merrill,
    William L. Sheppard, and Henry L. Stephens among others;
    engraved by John Andrew and Son.

Other Printings: Lee & Shepard; Charles T. Dillingham / Lee &
    Shepard; Lee, Shepard & Dillingham.

References: Hamilton. Early American book illustrators,
    #1856.

Locations: CtY, MWA, MnU, NHD, NN, WM

                            1876

100. "The amateur detective."

    Appeared serially in Munro's Girls and Boys of America
    25 March - 15 July 1876.

    This title has not been located in book form.

101. Living too fast: or, The confessions of a bank officer
        by William T. Adams. Lee & Shepard, c1876.

    Copyright #11744 dated October 18, 1876, granted to Lee &
    Shepard. Two copies deposited at LC on October 18, 1876.

    "With these two volumes [In-doors and out and Living too
    fast] the publisher will commence the issue of 'The
    Household Library' intending to embrace a series of
    attractive and wholesome romances, for the family
    circle." Publishers Weekly Book Fair Supplement 1876.

    Listed as "...just published." Publishers Weekly
    (28 October 1876).

Illustrations: Anonymous.

Reviews: "This is a most entertaining story, and it also
    carries with it an excellent moral, self-evident to
    almost any reader. It is beautifully printed and
    graphically illustrated. The scene of the story is
    laid in Boston; and the author's experience with his
    mother-in-law is very readable, as is also his reckless
    expenditures for his wife's sake, he harboring a false
    pride which inclined him to think that keeping up appear-
    ances was nearly the whole life. If you want to place a
    thoroughly entertaining and profitable book in your
    library, do not fail to send to the publishers of this
    charming story, who will promptly furnish it on receipt
    of the price." Boston Cultivator. [per L&S ad].

    "Here is the last and best work of that instructive author.
    It is full of incidents of a fast life, the expedients to
    keep up appearances, resulting in crime, remorse, and the
    evil opinion of all good men. The narrative is replete
    with startling situations, temptations, and all that makes
    up a thrilling story, in the semblance of an autobiography
    well rendered, sprightly, pathetic, with a dash of sensa-
    tion." [L&S ad].

    Also reviewed in Independent 28 (16 November 1876): 8.

References: Wright III, #23.

Other Printings: Lee & Shepard (THE HOUSEHOLD LIBRARY v.2) /
    Lee & Shepard; Charles T. Dillingham / Lothrop, Lee &
    Shepard / Research Publications (WRIGHT AMERICAN FICTION
    v.3 [1876-1900] reel A-3 no.23).

Locations: CSmH, CtY, DLC, FTS, IDekN, MB, MWA, MnU, NHD, Nh

102.   Vine and olive: or, Young America in Spain and Portugal.
        A story of travel and adventure by William T. Adams.
        Lee & Shepard, c1876. YOUNG AMERICA ABROAD 2nd series
        v.5.

    Copyright #12599 dated November 13, 1876, granted to
    William T. Adams. Two copies deposited at LC on November
    21, 1876. Preface dated October 19, 1876.

Illustrations: Alfred R. Waud and Charles S. Reinhart.

Reviews: "...Contains the history of the Academy Squadron
    during the cruise along the shores of Spain and Portugal
    and the travels of the students in the Peninsula. Full
    of amusement and instruction, and written upon the same
    plan as the previous volume of this well known series."
    Publishers Weekly 10 (2 December 1876): 947.

    Also reviewed in New England Journal of Education 4 (9

December 1876): 263.

Other Printings: Lee & Shepard; Charles T. Dillingham (YOUNG
    AMERICA ABROAD) / Lothrop, Lee & Shepard (OLIVER OPTIC
    SERIES #45; YOUNG AMERICA ABROAD).

Locations: CtY, CSmH, DLC, FTS, FU, IDekN, MB, MWA, MWalB,
    MiEM, MnU, MsHAu, NHD, NN, Nh, OAU, OC, PP, PPiU, TxU,
    ViU

1877

103. Out west: or, Roughing it on the Great Lakes. Lee &
    Shepard, c1877. GREAT WESTERN SERIES v.2.

    Copyright #5120 dated April 28, 1877. Two copies
    deposited at LC on May 9, 1877. Preface dated
    November 10, 1876.

Illustrations: Alfred R. Waud; engraved by John Andrew and
    Son.

Reviews: Independent 29 (17 May 1877): 10.

Other Printings: Lee & Shepard; Charles T. Dillingham (GREAT
    WESTERN SERIES) / Lothrop, Lee & Shepard (GREAT WESTERN
    SERIES).

References: Hamilton. Early American book illustrators,
    #1265a.

Locations: DLC, FTS, FU, KU, MB, MWalB, MnU, NHD, Nh, NN,
    OBgU, OC, PP, ViU, WM

104. "Nothing but a boy."

    Originally appeared serially in New York Weekly July 16,
    1877 through ?? Reprinted in Good News December 20,
    1890 - March 28, 1891.

    This title has not been located in book form.

105. Just his luck. Lee & Shepard, c1877.

    Copyright #12624 dated November 1, 1877, granted to
    Lee & Shepard. Two copies deposited at LC on November
    19, 1877. Copyright renewal #123203 dated August 5,
    1905 granted to Alice Adams Russell.

Illustrations: Frank T. Merrill.

Other Printings: Caldwell / Lee & Shepard (AMERICAN BOYS'
    SERIES #25) / Lee & Shepard; Charles T. Dillingham (OUR
    BOYS' PRIZE LIBRARY) / Lothrop, Lee & Shepard (AMERICAN

BOYS' SERIES #25; OLIVER OPTIC SERIES #50).

Locations: DLC, FU, MWalB, MnU, OC, PP, ViU

106. Isles of the sea: or, Young America homeward bound.
      A story of travel and adventure by William T. Adams.
      Lee & Shepard, c1877. YOUNG AMERICA ABROAD 2nd
      series v.6.

   Copyright #14026 dated December 3, 1877, granted to William T. Adams. Two copies deposited at LC on December 4,
   1877. Copyright #A126234 granted for renewal in 1905.
   Preface dated November 3, 1877.

Description: "...in the pursuit of knowledge they [the
   students] visit the Madeira Islands, the Canaries...Mr.
   Tom Speers is the central figure...Tom is a high-toned
   young man, as are all the other characters with whom the
   young reader is at all likely to sympathize..." [preface].

Illustrations: Anonymous; engraved by John Andrew.

Reviews: "...contains the history of the Academy Squadron
   during its voyage 'homeward bound' across the Atlantic.
   The title of the book indicates the line of travel taken
   by the students, the Madeira Islands, the Canaries, the
   Azores, the Bermudas, and the Cape Verd Islands, being
   visited by the different vessels of the fleet. The
   little volume is replete with geographical and historical
   information and has a very satisfactory hero, who figures
   in many odd and out of-the-way adventures." Publishers
   Weekly 12 (15 December 1877): 824.

Other Printings: Lee & Shepard; Charles T. Dillingham (YOUNG
   AMERICA ABROAD) / Lothrop, Lee & Shepard (YOUNG AMERICA
   ABROAD).

Locations: CSmH, CtY, DLC, FU, IDekN, KU, MB, MWalB, MiEM,
   MnU, MsHAu, NHD, NN, Nh, OAU, OC, PP, PPiU, TxU, ViU

1878

107. Lake breezes: or, The cruise of the Sylvania. Lee &
      Shepard, c1878. GREAT WESTERN SERIES v.3.

   Copyright #11720 dated October 10, 1878, granted to William T. Adams. Two copies deposited at LC on October 24,
   1878. Copyright renewal #A150324. Preface dated August
   1, 1878.

Description: "...the hero who has done duty for the two
   preceding stories again appears...The story is mostly a
   record of a yachting cruise on the Great Lakes. This is
   old-fashioned, orthodox story telling; but, after all,

it is the only safe method." [preface].

Illustrations: Frank T. Merrill.

Reviews: "Lake Breezes...depicts the inevitably successful
young hero disporting himself in a steam yacht on the
great Western lakes, pursuing, in the first place, some
stolen securities, and after their recapture, being pur-
sued in turn by the robbed robber. The end hints at his
succession to an English baronetcy - particulars left for
a succeeding volume. The book is very improbable, very
exciting, and boys are almost certain to like it."
Literary World 9 (December 1878): 107.

"...It is rich in adventure and incidents, the chief object
of the young yachtsman being to chase another steam-yacht,
the twin sister of the one commanded by 'Captain Alick' of
which readers of the other volumes have heard."
Publishers Weekly 14 (2 November 1878): 539.

Other Printings: Lee & Shepard; Charles T. Dillingham (GREAT
WESTERN SERIES) / Lothrop, Lee & Shepard (GREAT WESTERN
SERIES).

Locations: DLC, FU, KU, MB, MWalB, MnU, MoS, MsHAu, NHD, NN,
OBgU, OC, PP, TxU, ViU, WM

1879

108. "The pink of the Pacific: or, The adventures of a
      stowaway."

This story was sold to Beadle in 1879.

Originally appeared serially in the Young New Yorker v.1
#25 (10 May 1879) - end of volume. It was announced that
the story would be continued in the [New York] Saturday
Journal v.10 #483, but it was not. Instead, it appeared
in the New York Saturday Journal v.10 #481-484 (31 May -
21 June 1879) in its entirety. It then appeared serially
in The Banner Weekly v.2 #58-71 (22 December 1883 - 22
March 1884). The story was reprinted in the same magazine
v.8 #380-393 (22 February - 24 May 1890). The Banner
Weekly reprinted the story a third time, this time with a
new sub-title, Running down the kidnappers, v.14 #706-720
(23 May - 29 August 1896).

This title has not been located in book form.

109. Going south: or, Yachting on the Atlantic coast. Lee &
      Shepard, c1879. GREAT WESTERN SERIES v.4.

Copyright #16833 dated December 13, 1879, granted to
William T. Adams. Two copies deposited at LC on December

13, 1879. Copyright renewal #A188237 dated 1907. Preface dated October 18, 1879.

Description: "The hero of the three preceding volumes is the principal character of this one;...he still maintains his good character, and is ever ready to render a kindly and Christian service, even to an enemy." [preface].

Illustrations: Alfred R. Waud.

Other Printings: Lee & Shepard; Charles T. Dillingham (GREAT WESTERN SERIES) / Lothrop, Lee & Shepard (GREAT WESTERN SERIES).

Locations: CSmH, DLC, FTS, FU, MB, MWalB, MnU, MsHAu, NHD, NN, Nh, OAU, OC, PP, TxU, ViU, WM

1880

110. "Minding his own business."

Originally appeared serially in Golden Days for Boys and Girls v.1 #20-32 (17 July - 9 October 1880); reprinted in Golden Days for Boys and Girls v.9 #23-35 (5 May - 28 July 1888).

This title has not been located in book form.

111. Down south: or, Yacht adventures in Florida. Lee & Shepard, c1880. GREAT WESTERN SERIES v.5.

Copyright #17409 dated November 15, 1880, granted to William T. Adams. Two copies deposited at LC on November 24, 1880. Copyright renewal #A214610 dated 1908. Preface dated August 25, 1880.

Description: "The action of the story is confined entirely to Florida...the same characters are again presented... The hero is as straightforward, resolute, and self reliant as ever. His yacht adventures consist of various excursions on the St. Johns River...with a run across to Indian River...to the Lake Country of Florida." [preface].

Illustrations: Anonymous.

Reviews: "The scene of this story is laid in Florida entirely, which would seem to make it out of place in a series of this name; but on reading it we find there is no misnomer. This author's books are popular and this volume will doubtless be widely read. The next volume of this series will take the hero of this story on a cruise in the Gulf of Mexico and up the Mississippi, into the heart of the 'West.'" New England Journal of Education 12 (6 January 1881): 10.

Also reviewed in Independent 33 (13 January 1881): 12.

Other Printings: Lee & Shepard; Charles T. Dillingham (GREAT
   WESTERN SERIES) / Lothrop, Lee & Shepard (GREAT WESTERN
   SERIES).

Locations: CSmH, DLC, FTS, FU, KU, MB, MWalB, MiEM, MnU,
   MsHAu, NHD, NN, Nh, OAU, OBgU, OC, PP, TxU, ViU, WM

112. "Lost-on island."

   Originally appeared serially in Golden Days for Boys and
   Girls v.1 #38 - v.2 #12 (20 November 1880 - 26 February
   1881); reprinted in Golden Days for Boys and Girls v.18
   #45 - v.19 #7 (25 September 1897 - 1 January 1898).

   This title has not been located in book form.

                         1881

113. The young folks' Robinson Crusoe: or, The adventures
      of an Englishman who lived alone for five years on
      an island of the Pacific Ocean. By A Lady; edited
      by William T. Adams (Oliver Optic). Lee & Shepard,
      c1881.

   Copyright #11077 dated July 16, 1881 granted to Lee &
   Shepard. Two copies deposited at LC on October 3, 1881.

Description: "...The Young Folks' Robinson Crusoe is here
   represented as an amiable and well-educated youth, early
   trained to habits of observation and reflection, and
   capable of pure and exalted feelings of religion, - a
   hero, in short, whom children may safely love and admire,
   yet not faultless, or they could not sympathize with him."
   [preface].

Reviews: American (Weekly) 3 (10 December 1881): 138;
   The Californian 4 (December 1881): 537; Literary World 12
   (3 December 1881): 450-51; Nation 32 (24 November 1881):
   419.

   Originally published with title: "The children's Robinson
   Crusoe." The pseudonym, "A Lady," is attributed to Eliza
   Ware Rotch Farrar 1791-1870. (Yale University catalog
   information).

Locations: CtY, MB

114. Up the river: or, Yachting on the Mississippi. Lee &
      Shepard, c1881. GREAT WESTERN SERIES v.6.

Copyright #12901 dated August 22, 1891, granted to William T. Adams. Two copies deposited at LC on September 15, 1881. Preface dated June 1, 1881.

Description: "The events of the story occur on the coast of Florida, in the Gulf of Mexico, and on the Mississippi River. The volume and the series close with the return of the hero, by a route not often taken by tourists, to his home in Michigan." [preface].

Illustrations: Anonymous.

Reviews: Independent 34 (12 January 1882): 11.

Other Printings: Lee & Shepard; Charles T. Dillingham (GREAT WESTERN SERIES) / Lothrop, Lee & Shepard (GREAT WESTERN SERIES).

Locations: CSmH, DLC, FTS, FU, MB, MnU, MsHAu, NHD, NN, Nh, OAU, OC, PP, WM

115. Building himself up: or, The cruise of the "Fish Hawk."

Copyright granted to James Elverson in 1881.

Originally appeared serially in Golden Days for Boys and Girls v.2 #42-52 (24 September - 17 December 1881). Reprinted in Golden Days for Boys and Girls v.17 #21-31 (11 April - 20 June 1896).

Published in book form by Lothrop, Lee & Shepard April 1, 1910.

Illustrations: Lewis J. Bridgman.

Other Printings: Street & Smith (ALGER SERIES #142; NEW MEDAL LIBRARY #523).

Variant Titles: Building himself up: or, A fight for right. (ALGER SERIES).

Locations: DLC, PP, ViU

116. "Beau Gray: or, Getting his living."

Copyright #20122 dated December 27, 1881, granted to the Boston Daily Globe. Two copies deposited at LC on February 8, 1882.

Appeared serially in the Boston Daily Globe 2 January - 4 February 1882.

This title has not been located in book form.

1882

117. Oliver Optic's annual: stories, poems, and pictures for
      little men and women by the best authors and artists.
      Russell Publishing Co., 1889-1892.

Other Printings: Estes & Lauriat / also published in London
    from 1889-1892.

Locations: DLC, FU, KU, NN, PPiU

118. Our little ones and the nursery: illustrated stories and
      poems for little people.

      Edited by Oliver Optic 1882-1892.

Dates: November 1880 - March 1899 (v.1 #1 - v.19 #5).
Editors: William Taylor Adams (1882?-1892); Lawrence Elkus
    (1893-1899).
Publishers: Russell Publishing Co., Boston (1880-1899).
References: R. Gordon Kelly. Children's periodicals of the
    United States. Westport, CT: Greenwood Press, 1983.
    Betty L. Lyons. "A history of children's secular magazines
    published in the United States from 1789-1899. (Ph.D.
    dissertation, Johns Hopkins University, 1942).

Frequent Contributors: Clara Doty Bates, George S. Burleigh,
    Palmer Cox, Sophie May, Emily Huntington Miller, Laura E.
    Richards, Margaret E. Sangster, and Kate Tannatt Woods.

Frequent Illustrators: Frederick Stuart Church, Frank T.
    Merrill, J.H. Moser, and A. Burnham Shute. Illustrations
    were of prime importance in this magazine and the depart-
    ment was under the direction of George T. Andrew.

Features: Common themes of stories and illustrations were
    animals, nature, loving parents, and faithful friends.

Other information: Aimed at children from three to nine years
    of age, the content and format of Our Little Ones and The
    Nursery differed considerably from earlier Oliver Optic
    editorial efforts. Adams's contributions to Our Little
    Ones were rare, unlike the numerous serializations which
    appeared in The Student and Schoolmate, and later, Oliver
    Optic's Magazine.

Locations: DLC, FU, ME, MWA, MoS, MsHAu, NN, OC, PP

119. "Dunn Brown and his double."

      Copyright #5905 dated April 14, 1882, granted to the
      Russell Publishing Co. Two copies deposited at LC on
      July 28, 1882.

Appeared serially in the Boston Weekly Globe 25 April –
23 May 1882.

This title has not been located in book form.

120. All adrift: or, The Goldwing club. Lee & Shepard,
        c1882. BOAT-BUILDER SERIES v.1.

Copyright #16499 dated October 5, 1882, granted to William
T. Adams. Two copies deposited at LC on November 3, 1882.
Preface dated August 21, 1882.

Illustrations: Anonymous.

Reviews: "...contains the adventures of a boy who is trying
    to do something to help support the family, but who finds
    himself all adrift in the world; he finally becomes a
    boatman, and so nearly all the scenes of the story are on
    the water; the boy shows not only that he can handle a
    boat, but that he has ingenuity and fertility of resources;
    the narrative of the hero's adventures contained in this
    volume is the introduction to the remaining volumes of the
    series, which will be made of practical value by the intro-
    duction of workshop mechanics, so that the readers will be
    taught to build a boat, a boathouse, to rig and sail a
    boat, etc." Publishers Weekly (11 November 1882): 635.

Other Printings: Lee & Shepard; Charles T. Dillingham (BOAT-
    BUILDER SERIES) / Lothrop, Lee & Shepard (AMERICAN BOYS'
    SERIES #95; BOAT-BUILDER SERIES; OLIVER OPTIC SERIES #46).

Locations: CSmH, CtY, DLC, FTS, FU, GEU, MB, MWalB, MnU,
    MsHAu, NHD, NN, Nh, OC, PP, TxU, WM

121. "Lyon Hart: or, Adrift in the world."

Copyright #20405 dated December 1, 1882, granted to James
Elverson. Two copies deposited at LC on December 1, 1882.
Copyright renewal #543 dated January 25, 1910.

Appeared serially in Golden Days for Boys and Girls v.4
#1-12 (9 December 1882 - 24 February 1883). Reprinted in
Golden Days for Boys and Girls v.17 #45 - v.18 #4 (26
September - 12 December 1896).

Published in book form by Lothrop, Lee & Shepard on
April 1, 1910 with title Lyon Hart's heroism (183).

1883

122. "Louis Chiswick: or, Going with the current."

Appeared serially in Golden Days for Boys and Girls v.4

#20-31 (21 April - 7 July 1883). Reprinted in Golden
Days for Boys and Girls v.18 #4-15 (12 December 1896 -
27 February 1897).

Copyright #9607 dated May 24, 1883, granted to James
Elverson. Two copies deposited at LC on May 24, 1883.
Copyright renewal #917 dated May 21, 1910, granted to
Alice Adams Russell.

Published in book form by Lothrop, Lee & Shepard on
April 1, 1910 with title Louis Chiswick's mission: or,
Going with the current (182).

123.   "Royal Tarr: or, Learning to live."

Copyright #12787 dated July 12, 1883, granted to James
Elverson. Two copies deposited at LC on July 12, 1883.
Copyright renewal #1914 dated June 21, 1911.

Appeared serially in Golden Days for Boys and Girls v.4
#33-44 (21 July - 6 October 1883). Reprinted in Golden
Days for Boys and Girls v.18 #18-29 (20 March - 5 June
1897).

Published in book form by Lothrop, Lee & Shepard on April
1, 1910 with title Royal Tarr's pluck: or, Learning to
live (184).

124.   Making a man of himself: or, Right makes might.

Originally appeared serially in The Golden Argosy 20
October 1883 - 26 January 1884.

Copyright #11138 dated May 16, 1885, granted to the Globe
Newspaper Co. No record of deposit.

Published in book form by Lothrop, Lee & Shepard
on April 11, 1911.

Illustrations: John Goss.

Other Printings: Street & Smith (ALGER SERIES #145; NEW MEDAL
    LIBRARY #559).

Variant Titles: Making a man of himself: or, His single-
    handed victory. (ALGER SERIES).

Locations: GEU, NN

125.   Snug Harbor: or, The Champlain mechanics. Lee &
        Shepard, c1883. BOAT-BUILDER SERIES v.2.

Copyright #19305 dated October 20, 1883, granted to Wil-

liam T. Adams. Two copies deposited at LC on October 20,
1883. Preface dated August 20, 1883.

Illustrations: Frank T. Merrill.

Reviews: "Dory Donwood [sic], who was the hero of the initial
    volume of this series, is again presented with many new
    characters. Like the former volume, the scene is laid on
    Lake Champlain and its shores. The Beach Hill Industrial
    School makes a beginning in this book, and its pupils are
    gathered together in the school room and the workshop.
    The author goes into details as far as possible of the
    work done by the Champlain mechanics; he aims to create
    an interest in carpentry and machinists' work."
    Publishers Weekly (1 December 1883): 832.

    "The author makes a great mistake in thinking to propi-
    tiate his boy-readers by a little sensation mixed with
    his advice, and the first twelve chapters of the book,
    dealing with robberies, murder, and 'rows,' which have
    nothing to do with boat-building except that the 'rows'
    take place on a lake, are very poor reading for anybody."
    Critic 3 (15 December 1883): 510.

    Also reviewed in American (Weekly) 7 (17 November 1883):
    90.

Other Printings: Lee & Shepard; Charles T. Dillingham (BOAT-
    BUILDER SERIES) / Lothrop, Lee & Shepard (BOAT-BUILDER
    SERIES).

Locations: CSmH, CtY, DLC, FTS, FU, IDekN, KU, MB, MWalB,
    MnU, MoS, MsHAu, NHD, NN, Nh, OBgU, OC, PP

1884

126. The professor's son: or, The triumphs of a young athlete.

Copyright #11922 dated June 12, 1884, granted to James
Elverson. Two copies deposited at LC on June 12, 1884.
Copyright renewal #2550 dated January 29, 1912.

Originally appeared serially in Golden Days for Boys and
Girls v.5 #29-40 (21 June - 6 September 1884). Reprinted
in Golden Days for Boys and Girls v.20 #31-42 (17 June -
2 September 1899).

Published in book form by Lothrop, Lee & Shepard on April
1, 1910.

Illustrations: Lyle T. Hammond.

Other Printings: Street & Smith (ALGER SERIES #139; NEW MEDAL
    LIBRARY #546).

Variant Titles: The professor's son: or, Against all
    obstacles. (ALGER SERIES).

Locations: DLC

127. Every inch a boy.

    Copyright #18437 dated August 30, 1884, granted to Frank
    A. Munsey. Two copies deposited at LC on September 11,
    1884. Copyright renewal #2658 dated January 29, 1912.

    Originally appeared serially in The Golden Argosy 30
    August - 8 November 1884.

    Published in bock form by Lothrop, Lee & Shepard on April
    1, 1911.

Other Printings: Street & Smith (ALGER SERIES #127; NEW
    MEDAL LIBRARY #565).

Variant Titles: Every inch a boy: or, Fighting for a hold.
    (ALGER SERIES).

Locations: PP

128. Square and compasses: or, Building the house. Lee &
        Shepard, c1884. BOAT-BUILDER SERIES v.3.

    Copyright #20883 dated October 17, 1884, granted to Lee &
    Shepard. No record of copies being deposited. Preface
    dated August 20, 1884.

Illustrations: William L. Sheppard.

Reviews: "The third volume in the series devoted to the
    object of interesting young people in the mechanic arts.
    By means of a well-told story much practical instruction
    is given, and the results of good discipline in schools
    of every kind are specially dwelt upon. The characters
    are those of the last book, with a few successful
    additions." Publishers Weekly (1 November 1884): 612.

    "...the adventures of the students of an industrial
    school, and the endeavor is made to teach the value of
    discipline, and 'to interest young people in the mechanic
    arts.' The author is more successful, however, in
    describing their contests with the 'ruffianly' Chester-
    field boys and Topovers, than in making either interest-
    ing or easily intelligible their method of framing a
    building." Nation 39 (6 November 1884): 404.

    Also reviewed in American (Weekly) 9 (29 December 1884):
    169-70.

Other Printings: Lee & Shepard; Charles T. Dillingham (BOAT-
    BUILDER SERIES) / Lothrop, Lee & Shepard (BOAT-BUILDER
    SERIES).

Locations: CtY, DLC, FU, GEU, IDekN, MB, MWalB, MnU, MsHAu,
    NHD, NN, Nh, OBgU, OC, PP, TxU, WM

1885

129. The adventures of a midshipman. Glasgow: J.S. Marr &
    Sons, c1885.

Reprint of The Yankee Middy (44).

Other Printings: Ward & Lock, London.

Locations: DLC

130. "Fighting for his own."

    Appeared serially in Golden Days for Boys and Girls v.6
    #25-36 (23 May - 8 August 1885). Reprinted in Golden
    Days for Boys and Girls v.21 #5-16 (16 December 1899 -
    3 March 1900).

    Published in book form by Lothrop, Lee & Shepard on
    October 1, 1910, with title Striving for his own (185).

131. Stem to stern: or, Building the boat. Lee & Shepard,
    c1885. BOAT-BUILDER SERIES v.4.

    Copyright #19282 dated September 12, 1885, granted to
    William T. Adams. Two copies deposited at LC on October
    5, 1885. Preface dated August 17, 1885.

Description: "...largely a story of adventure on Lake Cham-
    plain and its shores. A new character is introduced as
    the leading spirit of the story...Though he is peaceful
    and submissive under ordinary circumstances, with none
    of the swellish importance of many boys of his years, he
    is not a milk-and-water youth, and has pluck and strength
    enough to 'stand up' for those whom misfortune has placed
    under his protection." [preface].

Illustrations: Frank T. Merrill.

Other Printings: Lee & Shepard; Charles T. Dillingham (BOAT-
    BUILDER SERIES) / Lothrop, Lee & Shepard (BOAT-BUILDER
    SERIES).

Locations: CtY, DLC, FU, GEU, MB, MWalB, MnU, MsHAu, NHD, NN,
    Nh, OBgU, OC, PP, TxU, WM

132. His own helper: or, Doing for himself.

Copyright #25936 dated December 10, 1885, granted to
James Elverson. Two copies deposited at LC on December
10, 1885. Copyright renewal #4062 dated March 12, 1913
and #4429 dated August 20, 1913.

Originally appeared serially in Golden Days for Boys and
Girls v.7 #3-14 (19 December 1885 - 6 March 1886).
Reprinted in Golden Days for Boys and Girls v.22 #18-29
(16 March - 1 June 1901).

Published in book form by Lothrop, Lee & Shepard on April
1, 1911.

Illustrations: Lyle T. Hammond.

Other Printings: Street & Smith (ALGER SERIES #125; NEW MEDAL
    LIBRARY #571).

Variant Titles: His own helper: or, By sheer pluck. (ALGER
    SERIES); His own helper: or, Stout arm and true heart.
    (NEW MEDAL LIBRARY; Lothrop, Lee & Shepard).

Locations: Nh

                            1886

133. All taut: or, Rigging the boat. Lee & Shepard,
      c1886. BOAT-BUILDER SERIES v.5.

Copyright #21369 dated September 24, 1886, granted to
William T. Adams. Two copies deposited at LC on September 24, 1886. Preface dated 1886.

Description: "Nearly all the characters presented, and all
    who take prominent parts in the story, have been intro-
    duced in the preceding volumes. The principal of the
    Beech Hill Industrial School entertains some doubts in
    regard to the principle upon which he has been conducting
    the institution and brings about a partial change in its
    character." [preface].

Illustrations: Anonymous.

Reviews: Critic ns 6 (20 November 1886): 249.

Other Printings: Lee & Shepard; Charles T. Dillingham (BOAT-
    BUILDER SERIES) / Lothrop, Lee & Shepard (BOAT-BUILDER
    SERIES).

Locations: CtY, DLC, FTS, FU, GEU, IDekN, MB, MWalB, MnU,
    MsHAu, NHD, NN, Nh, OC, PP, WM

1887

134. "Kit Dunstable: or, A watch for nothing."

Copyright #340 dated January 6, 1887, granted to James
Elverson. Two copies deposited at LC on January 6, 1887.
Copyright renewal #5753 dated October 10, 1914.

Appeared serially in Golden Days for Boys and Girls
v.8 #7-18 (15 January - 2 April 1887). Reprinted in
Golden Days for Boys and Girls v.21 #35-46 (14 July -
29 September 1900).

Published in book form by Lothrop, Lee & Shepard on
April 1, 1911, with title Honest Kit Dunstable (186).

135. Always in luck: or, Working for a living.

Copyright #3794 dated February 16, 1887, granted to
Frank A. Munsey. Two copies deposited at LC on February
16, 1887. Copyright renewal #5752 dated October 10, 1914.

Originally appeared serially in The Golden Argosy 15
January - 23 April 1887.

Published in book form by Lothrop, Lee & Shepard on April
1, 1912.

Other Printings: Street & Smith (ALGER SERIES #129; NEW MEDAL
    LIBRARY #634).

136. Nature's young noblemen by Brooks McCormick.

Originally appeared serially in The Golden Argosy 26
February - 4 June 1887.

Copyright #29164 dated October 13, 1888, granted to Frank
A. Munsey. Two copies deposited at LC on June 7, 1889.

Published in book form by Street & Smith and David McKay.

Other Printings: Federal (BOYS OWN LIBRARY) / International
    (ST. NICHOLAS SERIES) / Lovell (LEATHERCLAD TALES #6) /
    McKay (THE BOYS' OWN LIBRARY) / Munsey (MUNSEY'S POPULAR
    SERIES #14) / Street & Smith (BOYS' OWN LIBRARY #78; MEDAL
    LIBRARY #56).

Variant Titles: Nature's young nobleman (THE BOYS' OWN
    LIBRARY; BOYS' OWN LIBRARY #78; MUNSEY'S POPULAR SERIES
    #14; ST. NICHOLAS SERIES).

Locations: DLC

137.   Three young silver kings.

Copyright #13248 dated May 19, 1887, granted to James
Elverson.   Two copies deposited at LC on May 20, 1887.
Copyright renewal #5754 dated October 10, 1914.

Originally appeared serially in Golden Days for Boys and
Girls v.8 #26-39 (28 May - 27 August 1887).   Reprinted in
Golden Days for Boys and Girls v.21 #46 - v.22 #6 (29
September - 22 December 1900).

Published in book form by Lothrop, Lee & Shepard on April
1, 1912.

Illustrations: H. Boylston Dummer.

Other Printings: Street & Smith (ALGER SERIES #144; NEW MEDAL
   LIBRARY #595).

Variant Titles: Three young silver kings: or, In search of
   treasure. (ALGER SERIES);   Three young silver kings: or,
   At fortune's call. (Lothrop, Lee & Shepard).

Locations: DLC, GEU, NN

138.   Ready about: or, Sailing the boat.   Lee & Shepard,
       c1887.   BOAT-BUILDER SERIES v.6.

Copyright #14077 dated May 31, 1887, granted to William
T. Adams.   Two copies deposited at LC on July 23, 1887.
Preface dated July 15, 1887.

Descriptions: "...new characters presented in the story are
   the members of 'The Nautifelers Club,' who are introduced
   to exhibit the contrast between young men of high aims
   and correct principles, and those who are inclined to live
   too fast, and have no fixed idea of duty to sustain and
   advance them in the battle of life...[this book's] tendency
   is to inculcate courage without rashness, and to show that
   a young man of high principles is not necessarily a coward
   and a milksop." [preface].

Illustrations: Copeland.

Reviews: "This concludes the twelfth series for young people
   written by 'Oliver Optic.'   The whole art of boat-building,
   boat-rigging, boat-managing, and boat-sailing has been
   taught by means of interesting stories...meant to teach
   other useful lessons of importance in shaping the young
   readers' lives and characters." Publishers Weekly (1
   October 1887): 478.

Other Printings: Lee & Shepard; Charles T. Dillingham (BOAT-
   BUILDER SERIES) / Lothrop, Lee & Shepard (BOAT BUILDER-
   SERIES).

Locations: CtY, DLC, FU, KU, MB, MWalB, MnU, MsHAu, NHD,
   NN, Nh, OC, PP, WM

139. How he won by Brooks McCormick.

Originally appeared serially in The Golden Argosy 15
October - 24 December 1887.

Copyright #18635 dated April 29, 1892, granted to United
States Book Co. No record of copies deposited. Copyright
renewal #A18288.

Other Printings: Federal (BOYS' OWN LIBRARY) / McKay (BOYS'
   OWN LIBRARY; FAMOUS ADVENTURE SERIES #5) / Street & Smith
   (BOYS' OWN LIBRARY #57; MEDAL LIBRARY #62).

Locations: DLC

140. "The young pilot of Lake Montoban."

Copyright #28486 dated November 2, 1887, granted to Frank
A. Munsey. No record of deposit. Copyright renewal #7017
dated October 11, 1915.

Appeared serially in The Golden Argosy 22 October - 19
November 1887.

Published in book form by Lothrop, Lee & Shepard on April
1, 1911 with title The young pilot (187).

141. The cruise of the "Dandy."

Originally appeared serially in The Golden Argosy 3 December 1887 - 10 March 1888.

Copyright #33593 dated December 23, 1887, granted to Frank
A. Munsey. Two copies deposited at LC on November 28,
1887. Copyright renewal #7020 dated October 11, 1915.

Published in book form by Lothrop, Lee & Shepard on
April 1, 1911.

Other Printings: Street & Smith (ALGER SERIES #141; NEW MEDAL
   LIBRARY #589).

Variant Titles: The cruise of the "Dandy": or, Doing his
   best. (ALGER SERIES).

Locations: GEU, KU

1888

142.   The casket of diamonds: or, Hope Everton's inheritance
        by Gayle Winterton.

    Originally appeared serially in The Golden Argosy 31 March
    - 14 July 1888.

    Copyright #18629 dated April 29, 1892, granted to the
    United States Book Co. No record of copies deposited.

Other Printings: American Publishers Corporation (BERKELEY
    SERIES) / Donohue (ADVENTURE AND JUNGLE SERIES #2) /
    Thompson and Thomas and C.C. Thompson Co.

Note: In book form, the author is listed as "Oliver Optic."

Locations: DLC, FU, MnU

143.   "The young reformer."

    Copyright #10192 dated April 7, 1888, granted to the
    Lorborn Publishing Co. of Baltimore, MD. Two copies
    deposited at LC on April 14, 1888.

    This title has not been located in either serialization
    or book form.

144.   The young hermit of Lake Minnetonka.

    Originally appeared serially in The Golden Argosy 19 May -
    8 September 1888.

    Copyright #17609 dated June 20, 1888, granted to Frank A.
    Munsey. Two copies deposited at LC on May 12, 1888.
    Copyright renewal #7018 dated October 11, 1915.

    Published in book form by Lothrop, Lee & Shepard on April
    1, 1912.

Other Printings: Street & Smith (ALGER SERIES #140; NEW MEDAL
    LIBRARY #603).

Variant Titles: The young hermit: or, What life gave him.
    (ALGER SERIES); The young hermit: or, Adventures afloat
    and ashore. (NEW MEDAL LIBRARY).

Locations: GEU, NN, PPiU

145.   Taken by the enemy. Lee & Shepard, c1888. THE BLUE AND
        THE GRAY SERIES v.1.

    Copyright #22923 dated August 9, 1888, granted to Lee &
    Shepard. Two copies deposited at LC on September 29, 1888.

Preface dated June 12, 1888.

Illustrations: A. Burnham Shute.

Reviews: "'Taken by the Enemy'...is as bright and entertaining as any work that Mr. Adams has yet put forth, and will
be as eagerly perused as any that has borne his name. It
would not be fair to the prospective reader to deprive him
of the zest which comes from the unexpected, by entering
into a synopsis of the story..." Boston Budget. [per L&S
ad].

"'Taken by the Enemy' has just come from the press, an
announcement that cannot but appeal to every healthy boy
from ten to fifteen years of age in the country. 'No
writer of the day,' says the Boston Commonwealth, 'whose
aim has been to hit the boyish heart, has been as successful as Oliver Optic. There is a period in the life of
every youth, just about the time that he is collecting
postage-stamps, and before his legs are long enough for a
bicycle, when he has the Oliver Optic fever. He catches
it by reading a few stray pages somewhere, and then there
is nothing for it but to let the matter take its course.
Relief comes only when the last page of the last book is
read; and then there are relapses whenever a new book
appears until one is safely on through the teens."
Literary News 9 (December 1888): 374. [per L&S ad].

"How many boys, we wonder, within the last twenty years,
have drawn their hopes of a glorious and conspicuous
career, from the lives of the heroes of the fertile Oliver
Optic Series... There is something remarkable in the fact
of an author outwriting his generation, and beginning on a
new and younger one; and the sight of this gay-colored
volume makes us regret the careless days when we saved our
small earnings to buy the latest issue of this entertaining author, and almost wish that our literary taste had
remained as juvenile as his faculty." Critic ns 10 (8
December 1888): 286.

"...examples of sturdy patriotism and uncomplaining
sacrifice. Oliver Optic has also joined this class of
book makers and has out in time for the holidays the first
of a projected series of six volumes of stories on Civil
War to be entitled Blue & Gray series." Chautauquan 9
(December 1888): 189.

"...This story is entirely one of adventure by sea, the
scene taking place chiefly on board the steam-yacht Belle-
vite, which the owner offers finally to the government for
the Union cause. In this volume he makes use of the yacht
to bring his family up from the south, where they are when
the war breaks out." Publishers Weekly (3 November 1888):
632.

Also reviewed in Independent 41 (29 August 1889): 1122,

1129.

Other Printings: Lee & Shepard; Charles T. Dillingham (THE
    BLUE AND THE GRAY SERIES) / Lothrop, Lee & Shepard (THE
    BLUE AND THE GRAY SERIES).

Locations: CSmH, CtY, DLC, FTS, FU, GEU, IDekN, KU, MB, MWalB,
    MiEM, MnU, MsHAu, NHD, NN, Nh, OAU, OC, PP, TxU, ViU, WM

146.   The giant islanders: a tale of adventure by Brooks
        McCormick.

    Originally appeared serially in The Golden Argosy 6
    October - 15 December 1888.

    Copyright #18638 dated April 29, 1892, granted to the
    United States Book Co. No record of copies deposited.

    Published in book form by Street & Smith and David McKay.

Other Printings: Federal (BOYS' OWN LIBRARY) / McKay (BOYS'
    OWN LIBRARY) / Street & Smith (BOYS' OWN LIBRARY #47;
    MEDAL LIBRARY #97).

Locations: DLC, MnU

147.   The prisoners of the cave.

    Copyright #31533 dated November 5, 1888, granted to Frank
    A. Munsey. No record of copies deposited. Copyright
    renewal #8252 dated April 19, 1916.

    Originally appeared serially in The Argosy 1 December
    1888 - 23 February 1889.

    Published in book form by Lothrop, Lee & Shepard on April
    1, 1912.

Illustrations: Donald Ross.

Other Printings: Street & Smith (ALGER SERIES #137; NEW MEDAL
    LIBRARY #615).

Variant Titles: The prisoners of the cave: or, By sheer will
    power. (ALGER SERIES).

Locations: IDekN, MsHAu

1889

148.   The rival battalions by Brooks McCormick.

    Originally appeared serially in The Argosy March 9 -

June 22, 1889.

Copyright #8949 dated March 2, 1891, granted to the
United States Book Co. of New York. Two copies deposited
at LC on March 2, 1891.

Published in book form by United States Book Co.
(LEATHERCLAD TALES #29).

Other Printings: Federal (BOYS' OWN LIBRARY) / McKay (THE
    BOYS' OWN LIBRARY) / Street & Smith (BOYS' OWN LIBRARY
    #93; MEDAL LIBRARY #79).

Locations: DLC

149. Within the enemy's lines. Lee & Shepard, c1889. THE
      BLUE AND THE GRAY SERIES v.2.

Copyright #15954 dated May 27, 1889, granted to Lee &
Shepard. Two copies deposited at LC on September 13,
1889. Preface dated May 2, 1889.

Illustrations: Copeland.

Reviews: "The ever popular Oliver Optic adds a second volume
    to his 'Blue and Gray Series' an account of some thrill-
    ing adventures... in the heat of the great Civil War.
    The descriptions are graphic and the action brisk and
    vigorous; just the kind of book in which a boy delights."
    Chautauquan 10 (December 1889): 378.

    "...this story opens at a more advanced stage of the
    Rebellion, and tells of a second and equally daring
    attempt of the Southerners to capture the yacht Bellevite
    ...The book is written from a northern standpoint, al-
    though there is nothing offensive to the southern side
    of the question." Publishers Weekly (5 October 1889):
    496.

    Also reviewed in Picayune 15 (December 1889): 11.

Other Printings: Lee & Shepard; Charles T. Dillingham (THE
    BLUE AND THE GRAY SERIES) / Lothrop, Lee & Shepard (THE
    BLUE AND THE GRAY SERIES).

Locations: DLC, FTS, FU, GEU, IDekN, KU, MB, MWalB, MiEM,
    MnU, MsHAu, NHD, NN, Nh, OBgU, OC, PP, TxU, ViU, WM

150. Holiday joys for bright girls and boys. Comprising
      stories, sketches and poems edited by Oliver Optic
      with entirely original illustrations by the best
      known American artists. R.S. Peale & Co., c1889.

Copyright #32798 dated October 29, 1889, granted to R.S.

Peale & Co. No record of copies deposited. Copyright
#35267 dated November 21, 1889, granted to N.D. Thompson
Publishing Co. No record of copies deposited.

151. Story and song. For all winter long. Comprising
      stories, sketches and poems for little people written
      expressly for this volume by one hundred famous
      authors. Edited by Oliver Optic with 370 entirely
      original illustrations drawn by the most celebrated
      American artists and engraved by George T. Andrew.
      R.S. Peale & Co., c1889.

      Copyright #32799 dated October 29, 1889, granted to R.S.
      Peale & Co. No record of copies deposited. Copyright
      #35266 dated November 21, 1889 granted to N.D. Thompson
      Publishing Co. No record of copies deposited.

152. The young actor: or, The solution of a mystery by Gayle
      Winterton.

      Originally appeared serially in The Argosy 2 November
      1889 - 15 February 1890.

      Copyright #41696 dated December 27, 1890, granted to the
      United States Book Co. Copies deposited at LC on Feb-
      ruary 16, 1891.

      Published in book form by United States Book Co.
      (LEATHERCLAD TALES #27).

Other Printings: Federal (BOYS' OWN LIBRARY) / McKay (THE
      BOYS' OWN LIBRARY) / Street & Smith (BOYS' OWN LIBRARY
      #127; MEDAL LIBRARY #105; NEW MEDAL LIBRARY #382) /
      Tait.

Locations: CSmH, DLC

                        1890

153. Among the missing.

      Originally appeared serially in The Argosy 18 January -
      17 May 1890.

      Copyright #3714 dated January 28, 1890, granted to Frank
      A. Munsey. Two copies deposited at LC on January 11,
      1890. Copyright renewal #10884 dated November 26, 1917.

      Published in book form by Lothrop, Lee & Shepard on April
      1, 1912.

Illustrations: Arthur C. Knapp.

Other Printings: Street & Smith (ALGER SERIES #124; NEW MEDAL
    LIBRARY #627).

Variant Titles: Among the missing: or, The boy they could not
    beat. (ALGER SERIES).

Locations: NN, PPiU

154. Little blossoms in the garden of home: or, Songs and
      poems for little folks by America's best writers.
      Edited by William T. Adams ("Oliver Optic"). With
      over two hundred exquisite original engravings by
      famous American artists.   Thayer, Merriam & Co.,
      c1890.

      Copyright #17400 dated May 28, 1890, granted to F.
      Oldach, Sr. Two copies deposited December 31, 1890.

Other Printings: E.R. Curtis & Co.

Locations: DLC, FU, PPiU

155. On the blockade. Lee & Shepard, c1890.   THE BLUE AND
      THE GRAY SERIES v.3.

      Copyright #23297 dated July 24, 1890, granted to Lee &
      Shepard. Two copies deposited at LC on September 6, 1890.
      Preface dated April 24, 1890.

Description: "Incidents are dated back to the War of the
    Rebellion, and located in the midst of its most stirring
    scenes on the Southern coast, where the naval operations
    of the United States contributed their full share to the
    final result..." [preface].

Illustrations: Lewis J. Bridgman.

Reviews: "A story for boys, in which the scenes are laid
    during the war for the Union. The characters have the
    destiny which always awaits them in this writer's books,
    and the incidents are selected for their interesting
    nature and their helpfulness to the story, as all
    incidents should be." Atlantic Monthly 47 (January 1891):
    132.

    "The books of this popular writer remind us of certain
    building blocks for children, the merit of which is that
    from only half-a-dozen kinds of blocks very many sorts of
    structures may be built. A considerable number of Oliver
    Optic's stories have the same half-dozen characters, with
    whom he builds his plots...The adult reader may raise his
    eyebrows a little at the preternaturally mature doings of
    a boy of eighteen placed in command of a man-of-war; but
    the younger and less critical reader sees no difficulties,

and will ardently desire to emulate the deeds of such a gallant hero." Literary World 21 (22 November 1890): 437.

Also reviewed in Godey's 122 (January 1891): 96.

Other Printings: Lee & Shepard; Charles T. Dillingham (THE BLUE AND THE GRAY SERIES) / Lothrop, Lee & Shepard (THE BLUE AND THE GRAY SERIES).

Locations: CSmH, DLC, FTS, FU, GEU, IDekN, MB, MWalB, MiEM, MnU, MsHAu, NHD, NN, Nh, OC, PP, PPiU, TxU, ViU, WM

1891

156. "A will of his own."

Copyright #4319 dated January 30, 1891, granted to The Toledo Blade Co. of Toledo, Ohio. No record of copies deposited.

This title has not been located in serialization or book form.

157. Stand by the Union. Lee & Shepard, c1891. THE BLUE AND THE GRAY SERIES v.4.

Copyright #25815 dated July 18, 1891, granted to Lee & Shepard. Two copies deposited at LC on September 2, 1891. Preface dated April 23, 1891.

Illustrations: Lewis J. Bridgman.

Reviews: Epoch 10 (6 November 1891): 215.

Other Printings: Lee & Shepard; Charles T. Dillingham (THE BLUE AND THE GRAY SERIES) / Lothrop, Lee & Shepard (THE BLUE AND THE GRAY SERIES).

Locations: CSmH, DLC, FTS, FU, GEU, IDekN, KU, MB, MWalB, MnU, MsHAu, NHD, NN, Nh, OC, PPiU, ViU, WM

158. A missing million: or, The adventures of Louis Belgrave. Lee & Shepard, c1891. ALL-OVER-THE-WORLD LIBRARY 1st series v.1.

Copyright #43455 dated December 3, 1891, granted to Lee & Shepard. Two copies deposited December 17, 1891. Preface dated November 20, 1891.

Description: "Louis Belgrave, the 'Millionaire at Sixteen,' is a young man of high aims and elevated character. Though he may do 'big things,' he will not lead his sympathizing reader astray." [preface].

Illustrations: Lewis J. Bridgman.

Other Printings: Lee & Shepard (AMERICAN BOYS' SERIES #62)
/ Lothrop, Lee & Shepard (ALL-OVER-THE-WORLD LIBRARY;
AMERICAN BOYS' SERIES #62; OLIVER OPTIC SERIES #31).

Locations: CtY, DLC, FTS, FU, IDekN, KU, MWalB, MnU, MsHAu,
NHD, NN, Nh, OC, PP, WM

1892

159. A millionaire at sixteen: or, The cruise of the
Guardian-Mother. Lee & Shepard, c1892. ALL-OVER-
THE-WORLD LIBRARY 1st series v.2.

Copyright #14559 dated April 2, 1892. Two copies deposited at LC on May 26, 1892. Preface dated March 5, 1892.

Illustrations: A. Burnham Shute.

Reviews: Critic ns 18 (16 July 1892): 31; Godey's 125
(August 1892): 195-96.

Other Printings: Lee & Shepard (AMERICAN BOYS' SERIES #63) /
Lothrop, Lee & Shepard (ALL-OVER-THE-WORLD LIBRARY;
AMERICAN BOYS' SERIES #63; OLIVER OPTIC SERIES #32).

Locations: CtY, DLC, FTS, FU, KU, MB, MWalB, MiEM, MnU, NHD,
NN, Nh, OAU, OC, PP, WM

160. Fighting for the right. Lee & Shepard, c1892. THE BLUE
AND THE GRAY SERIES v.5.

Copyright #34862X dated August 25, 1892, granted to Lee &
Shepard. Two copies deposited at LC on September 12,
1892. Preface dated April 18, 1892.

Description: "The incidents...are somewhat different from
most of those detailed in the preceding volumes...though
they all have the same patriotic tendency, and are car-
ried out with the same devotion to the welfare of the
nation as those which deal almost solely in deeds of arms
...No apology is necessary for placing the hero of the
story and his skillful associate in a position at a dis-
tance from the actual field of battle. They were 'Fighting for the Right' as they understood it..." [preface].

Illustrations: A. Burnham Shute.

Other Printings: Lothrop, Lee & Shepard (THE BLUE AND THE
GRAY SERIES).

Locations: CSmH, DLC, FTS, FU, GEU, IDekN, KU, MB, MWalB,
MiEM, MnU, MoS, MsHAu, NHD, NN, Nh, OC, PP, TxU, ViU, WM

161. A young knight-errant: or, Cruising in the West Indies.
      Lee & Shepard, c1892. ALL-OVER-THE-WORLD LIBRARY
      1st series v.3.

      Copyright #34863 dated August 25, 1892. Two copies
      deposited at LC on October 5, 1892. Preface dated Sep-
      tember 10, 1892.

Illustrations: Lewis J. Bridgman.

Other Printings: Lee & Shepard (AMERICAN BOYS' SERIES #64) /
      Lothrop, Lee & Shepard (ALL-OVER-THE-WORLD LIBRARY;
      AMERICAN BOYS' SERIES #64; OLIVER OPTIC SERIES #33).

Locations: DLC, FTS, FU, IDekN, KU, MB, MWalB, MnU, NHD, Nh,
      OC, PP

                              1893

162. Strange sights abroad: or, A voyage in European waters.
      Lee & Shepard, c1893. ALL-OVER-THE-WORLD LIBRARY
      1st series v.4.

      Copyright #13847 dated March 20, 1893, granted to Lee &
      Shepard. Two copies deposited at LC on April 15, 1893.
      Preface dated March 1893.

Illustrations: A. Burnham Shute.

Other Printings: Lee & Shepard (AMERICAN BOYS' SERIES #65) /
      Lothrop, Lee & Shepard (ALL-OVER-THE-WORLD LIBRARY;
      AMERICAN BOYS' SERIES #65; OLIVER OPTIC SERIES #34).

Locations: CtY, DLC, FTS, FU, KU, MB, MWalB, MnU, MsHAu,
      NHD, Nh, OAU, OC, WM

163. American boys afloat: or, Cruising in the Orient.
      Lee & Shepard, c1893. ALL-OVER-THE-WORLD LIBRARY
      2nd series v.1.

      Copyright #31370 dated July 3, 1893. Two copies deposited
      at LC on September 15, 1893. Preface dated August 15,
      1893.

Illustrations: Lewis J. Bridgman.

Other Printings: Lothrop, Lee & Shepard (ALL-OVER-THE-WORLD
      LIBRARY).

Locations: CSmH, CtY, DLC, FTS, FU, KU, MWalB, MnU, NHD, NN,
      Nh, OC, TxU, WM

164. A victorious union. Lee & Shepard, c1893. THE BLUE

AND THE GRAY SERIES v.6.

Copyright #36987 dated August 9, 1893, granted to Lee & Shepard. Two copies deposited at LC on September 16, 1893. Preface dated March 16, 1893.

Description: "In the present volume...he [the author] has endeavored to present to his readers, not only a hero who is brave, skilful [sic], and ready to give his life for his country, but one who is unselfishly patriotic; one who is not fighting for promotion and prize money, but to save the Union in whose integrity and necessity he believes as the safeguard and substance of American liberty." [preface].

Illustrations: Harry G. Burgess.

Reviews: "The works of this veteran writer are so dear to the heart of every American boy that they need no introduction. The present one is endowed with the same spirit and enthusiasm that characterized its predecessors, and is certain of its welcome." Dial 15 (1 December 1893): 350.

Other Printings: Lothrop, Lee & Shepard (THE BLUE AND THE GRAY SERIES).

Locations: CSmH, DLC, FTS, FU, GEU, IDekN, KU, MB, MWalB, MiEM, MnU, MsHAu, NHD, NN, Nh, OC, PP, PPiU, ViU, WM

165. The young navigators: or, The foreign cruise of the Maud. Lee & Shepard, c1893. ALL-OVER-THE-WORLD LIBRARY 2nd series v.2.

Copyright #42251 dated September 20, 1893. Two copies deposited at LC on November 13, 1893. Preface dated September 1893.

Illustrations: A. Burnham Shute.

Reviews: Book News Monthly 12 (January 1894): 214.

Other Printings: Lothrop, Lee & Shepard (ALL-OVER-THE-WORLD LIBRARY).

Locations: CSmH, DLC, FTS, FU, MnU, NHD, NN, Nh, OC, PP, PPiU, WM

1894

166. Up and down the Nile: or, Young adventurers in Africa. Lee & Shepard, c1894. ALL-OVER-THE-WORLD LIBRARY 2nd series, v.2.

Copyright #25454 dated May 21, 1894. Two copies
deposited at LC on June 8, 1894. Preface dated April 11,
1894.

Illustrations: A. Burnham Shute.

Other Printings: Lothrop, Lee & Shepard (ALL-OVER-THE-WORLD
    LIBRARY).

Locations: CtY, DLC, FTS, FU, GEU, IDekN, KU, MB, MnU, NHD,
    Nh, OC, WM

167. <u>Asiatic breezes: or, Students on the wing.</u> Lee &
      Shepard, c1894. ALL-OVER-THE-WORLD LIBRARY
      2nd series v.4.

Copyright #41378 dated September 10, 1894. Two copies
deposited at LC on October 27, 1894. Preface dated
September 30, 1894.

Illustrations: Anonymous.

Reviews: "The closing volume of the second series of 'All-
    Over-The-World Library' takes the travelers from Alex-
    andria to Cyprus and through the Suez Canal. There is
    much information given in conversational form concerning
    the places visited and the objects seen and a plenty of
    exciting incident and adventure." <u>Chautauquan</u> 20 (March
    1895): 762.

Other Printings: Lothrop, Lee & Shepard (ALL-OVER-THE-WORLD
    LIBRARY).

Locations: CSmH, CtY, DLC, FTS, FU, IDekN, KU, MB, MnU, NHD,
    NN, Nh, OC, WM

168. <u>Brother against brother: or, The war on the border.</u>
      Lee & Shepard, c1894. THE BLUE AND THE GRAY ON LAND
      SERIES v.1.

Copyright #41380 dated September 10, 1894, granted to
Lee & Shepard. Two copies deposited at LC on September
15, 1894. Preface dated July 4, 1894.

Description: "A New Hampshire family is transplanted to the
    southern part of one of the Border States just before the
    breaking out of the Great Rebellion...This first volume
    is devoted to bringing out the loyal element...in oppo-
    sition to the more demonstrative secession or neutral
    sentiment." [preface].

Illustrations: A. Burnham Shute.

Reviews: "A stirring narrative of the Civil War on the

Border, wholly free from partisan feeling, is the initial
volume of the new series of 'The Blue and the Gray,' by
the ever popular Oliver Optic." Chautauquan 20 (March
1895): 762.

Other Printings: Lothrop, Lee & Shepard (THE BLUE AND THE
   GRAY ON LAND SERIES).

Locations: CSmH, DLC, FTS, FU, GEU, IDekN, KU, MB, MnU,
   MsHAu, NHD, NN, Nh, OC, PP, ViU, WM

1895

169. Our little one's annual.

Published by Estes & Lauriat from 1895-1897.

170. In the saddle. Lee & Shepard, c1895. THE BLUE AND THE
   GRAY ON LAND SERIES v.2.

Copyright #14780 dated March 14, 1895, granted to Lee &
Shepard. Two copies deposited at LC on March 14, 1895.
Preface undated.

Description: "...this battalion enters upon active service.
   The same characters are presented in the uniform of
   cavalrymen, mounted on the fine equine stock of the
   plantation." [preface].

Illustrations: A. Burnham Shute.

Other Printings: Lothrop, Lee & Shepard (THE BLUE AND THE
   GRAY ON LAND SERIES).

Locations: CSmH, DLC, FU, GEU, KU, MB, MWalB, MiEM, MnU,
   MoS, MsHAu, NHD, NN, Nh, OC, PP, ViU, WM

171. Across India: or, Live boys in the Far East. Lee &
   Shepard, c1895. ALL-OVER-THE-WORLD LIBRARY 3rd
   series v.1.

Copyright #16551 dated March 23, 1895. Two copies
deposited at LC on June 13, 1895. Preface undated.

Illustrations: A. Burnham Shute.

Reviews: "Many boys accept a great amount of information if
   it is strung on the slightest thread of story, when they
   would not sit down and read the same facts told vividly
   in a well-written volume of travels. Oliver Optic's books
   are always popular with his boy public, and he does manage
   to convey a good deal of useful information in a palatable
   shape. 'Across India' has enough snakes and tigers in it

to form a good-sized menagerie; for this and other reasons
boys will delight in it." Literary World 26 (27 July
1895): 233.

Other Printings: Lothrop, Lee & Shepard (ALL-OVER-THE-WORLD
    LIBRARY).

Locations: DLC, FTS, KU, MB, MnU, NHD, NN, Nh, OC, WM

172. Half round the world: or, Among the uncivilized.
      Lee & Shepard, c1895. ALL-OVER-THE-WORLD LIBRARY
      3rd series v.2.

    Copyright #50192 dated October 3, 1895. Two copies
    deposited at LC on October 21, 1895. Preface undated.

Illustrations: A. Burnham Shute.

Reviews: "... It narrates the incidents and adventures of a
    party of young people on their own steamer. Primarily
    the objects of the books are to teach the youth history
    and geography, and we have hitherto commended these,
    but if they all contain as many errors as the present
    volume, they had better never been written...Oliver Optic
    must be in his dotage." Overland Monthly series 2 27
    (January 1896): 125-26.

Other Printings: Lothrop, Lee & Shepard (ALL-OVER-THE-WORLD
    LIBRARY).

Locations: FTS, KU, MB, MnU, NHD, NN, Nh, OC, WM

173. A lieutenant at eighteen. Lee & Shepard, c1895. THE
      BLUE AND THE GRAY ON LAND SERIES v.3.

    Copyright #50191 dated October 3, 1895, granted to Lee &
    Shepard. Two copies deposited at LC on November 11, 1895.
    Preface undated.

Description: "...Deck Lyon is promoted to the rank of
    lieutenant although he is only eighteen..." [preface].

Illustrations: A. Burnham Shute.

Other Printings: Lothrop, Lee & Shepard (THE BLUE AND THE
    GRAY ON LAND SERIES).

Locations: CSmH, DLC, FTS, FU, GEU, IDekN, KU, MB, MWalB,
    MnU, MsHAu, NHD, NN, Nh, OC, PP, ViU, WM

                        1896

174. "A trip around the world: a personal narrative" by

William T. Adams, [1896].

Unpublished 42 page story.

Locations: CtY, PP

175. On the staff. Lee & Shepard, c1896. THE BLUE AND THE
      GRAY ON LAND SERIES v.4.

   Copyright #53770 dated September 28, 1896, granted to
   Lee & Shepard. Two copies deposited at LC on September
   28, 1896. Preface undated.

Illustrations: A. Burnham Shute.

Other Printings: Lothrop, Lee & Shepard (THE BLUE AND THE
   GRAY ON LAND SERIES).

Locations: CSmH, DLC, FU, GEU, IDekN, MB, MnU, MsHAu, NHD,
   NN, Nh, OC, PP, PPiU, TxU, ViU, WM

176. Four young explorers: or, Sight-seeing in the tropics.
      Lee & Shepard, c1896. ALL-OVER-THE-WORLD LIBRARY
      3rd series v.3.

   Copyright #61147 dated November 7, 1896. Two copies
   deposited at LC on November 9, 1896. Preface undated.

Illustrations: Anonymous.

Other Printings: Lothrop, Lee & Shepard (ALL-OVER-THE-WORLD
   LIBRARY).

Locations: DLC, FTS, FU, IDekN, MB, MWalB, MnU, NHD, Nh, OC,
   PP

1897

177. Pacific shores: or, Adventures in eastern seas.
      Lee & Shepard, c1897. ALL-OVER-THE-WORLD LIBRARY
      3rd series v.4.

   Copyright #43925 dated August 3, 1897. No record of
   copies deposited. Preface undated.

Illustrations: A. Burnham Shute.

Other Printings: Lothrop, Lee & Shepard (ALL-OVER-THE-WORLD
   LIBRARY).

Locations: CtY, DLC, FTS, FU, IDekN, MB, MnU, NHD, NN, Nh, OC

178. **At the front.** Lee & Shepard, c1897. THE BLUE AND THE
      GRAY ON LAND SERIES v.5.

Copyright #43924 dated August 3, 1897, granted to Lee &
Shepard. Two copies deposited at LC on August 25, 1897.
Preface undated.

Description: "...a continuation of the narrative contained
    in the preceding books, wherein is given the history of
    the Riverlawn Regiment from the formation of the two
    companies as a squadron, in which it rendered its first
    service for the preservation of the Union, till in the
    present volume it becomes a full cavalry regiment of
    twelve companies, with three battalions, a colonel, a
    lieutenant-colonel and three majors." [preface].

Illustrations: A. Burnham Shute.

Other Printings: Lothrop, Lee & Shepard (THE BLUE AND THE
    GRAY ON LAND SERIES).

Locations: CtY, DLC, FU, GEU, IDekN, MB, MnU, MoS, MsHAu,
    NHD, NN, Nh, OBgU, PP, ViU, WM

1899

179. **An undivided union** completed by Edward Stratemeyer.
      Lee & Shepard, c1899. THE BLUE AND THE GRAY ON LAND
      SERIES v.6.

Copyright #24668 dated April 8, 1899, granted to Lee &
Shepard. Two copies deposited at LC on July 13, 1899.
Preface dated April 1, 1899.

Description: "...relates the adventures of the Riverlawn
    Cavalry...given an account of the operations around
    Murfreesboro, before Tullahoma, and through the bloody
    battles of Chickamauga, Chattanooga, Lookout Mountain,
    Missionary Ridge, and other contests leading up to
    Sherman's famous March to the Sea." [preface].

Illustrations: A. Burnham Shute.

Reviews: "At the time of his death, two years ago, W.T. Adams
    (Oliver Optic) had published one hundred and seven boys'
    books. He left unfinished a story which has been com-
    pleted by Edward Stratemeyer, along the lines indicated
    by the author's notes...Stories by this author are
    habitually clean, vigorous and admirably adapted to the
    readers for whom they are designed, and the present
    volume is no exception." Chautauquan 30 (December 1899):
    330.

This volume was completed by Edward Stratemeyer after
Adams' death in 1897.

"...There has been a constant demand that this unfinished concluding volume be prepared for publication, and Mr. Edward Stratemeyer...undertook the task of picking up the threads of the narrative and carrying it to such a conclusion as was evidently intended..." [Publishers' preface].

Other Printings: Lothrop, Lee & Shepard (THE BLUE AND THE GRAY ON LAND SERIES).

Locations: CSmH, CtY, DLC, FU, MB, MiEM, MnU, MsHAu, NHD, NN, Nh, OC, PP, TxU, ViU, WM

1902

180. Oliver Optic's new story book: or, Stories in rhyme and prose for little folks. By America's best writers. Edited by William T. Adams. Hurst, c1902.

Published as part of Hurst's FIRESIDE SERIES.

1907

181. "That Dillingham boy."

Appeared serially in American Boy November 1907 - February 1909.

This title has not been located in book form.

1910

182. Louis Chiswick's mission: or, Going with the current. Lothrop, Lee & Shepard, 1910.

Published in book form by Lothrop, Lee & Shepard on April 1, 1910.

See entry #122 for copyright information.

Illustrations: Louis D. Gowing.

Other Printings: Street & Smith (ALGER SERIES #138; NEW MEDAL LIBRARY #534).

Variant Titles: Louis Chiswick's mission: or, Up the ladder of success. (ALGER SERIES).

Originally appeared serially under title "Louis Chiswick: or, Going with the current." (122).

Locations: DLC, MsHAu, NN

183. <u>Lyon Hart's heroism.</u> Lothrop, Lee & Shepard, 1910.

Published in book form by Lothrop, Lee & Shepard on April 1, 1910.

See entry #121 for copyright information.

Other Printings: Street & Smith (ALGER SERIES #143; NEW MEDAL LIBRARY #528).

Variant Titles: <u>Lyon Hart's heroism: or, Courage wins.</u> (ALGER SERIES).

Originally appeared serially under title "Lyon Hart: or, Adrift in the world." (121).

Locations: GEU, NN

184. <u>Royal Tarr's pluck: or, Learning to live.</u> Lothrop, Lee & Shepard, 1910.

Published by Lothrop, Lee & Shepard on April 1, 1910.

See entry #123 for copyright information.

Illustrations: Louis D. Gowing.

Other Printings: Street & Smith (ALGER SERIES #136; NEW MEDAL LIBRARY #540).

Variant Titles: <u>Royal Tarr's pluck: or, The boy who fought fair.</u> (ALGER SERIES).

Originally appeared serially under title "Royal Tarr: or, Learning to live." (123).

Locations: GEU, MiEM

185. <u>Striving for his own.</u> Lothrop, Lee & Shepard, 1910.

Published in book form by Lothrop, Lee & Shepard on April 1, 1910.

See entry #130 for copyright information.

Other printings: Street & Smith (ALGER SERIES #146; NEW MEDAL LIBRARY #552).

Variant Titles: <u>Striving for his own: or, Working toward success.</u> (ALGER SERIES).

Originally appeared serially under title "Fighting for his own." (130).

Locations: NN

                              1911

186. <u>Honest Kit Dunstable.</u> Lothrop, Lee & Shepard, 1911.

      Published in book form by Lothrop, Lee & Shepard on April
      1, 1911.

      See entry #134 for copyright information.

Illustrations: Dwight C. Sturges.

Other Printings: Street & Smith (ALGER SERIES #126; NEW
      MEDAL LIBRARY #577).

Variant Titles: <u>Honest Kit Dunstable: or, The boy who earned
      money.</u> (ALGER SERIES).

      Originally appeared serially under title "Kit Dunstable:
      or, A watch for nothing." (134).

Locations: MsHAu, NN

187. <u>The young pilot.</u> Lothrop, Lee & Shepard, 1911.

      Published in book form by Lothrop, Lee & Shepard on April
      1, 1911.

      See entry #140 for copyright information.

Illustrations: J.W. Ferguson Kennedy.

Other Printings: Street & Smith (ALGER SERIES #128; HAPPY
      THOUGHT SERIES #5; NEW MEDAL LIBRARY #583).

Variant Titles: <u>The young pilot: or, Steady hand and true
      eye.</u> (HAPPY THOUGHT SERIES); <u>The Young Pilot: or, His
      own best protector.</u> (ALGER SERIES).

      Originally appeared serially under title "The young pilot
      of Lake Montoban." (140).

Locations: DLC, GEU, WM

                              1912

188. <u>Charades and pantomimes for school and home
      entertainment</u> ... with additions by Oliver
      Optic. DeWolfe & Fiske, c1912.

      A copy of this title has not been located.

189.   <u>Popular amusements for school and home</u> edited by
       Oliver Optic. DeWolfe & Fiske, c1912.

   A copy of this title has not been located.

AUTHOR SERIES

Listed below are all titles which were part of an original
series first issued by William T. Adams and Lee & Shepard.
The series names are in alphabetical order, with each title
in the original chronological order as they were published.
The number in parenthesis following the title refers to the
entry number in the CHRONOLOGICAL LIST.

1AS   ALL-OVER-THE-WORLD LIBRARY - First series

1AS.1   A missing million: or, The adventures of Louis
        Belgrave (153)
1AS.2   A millionaire at sixteen: or, The cruise of the
        "Guardian-Mother" (159)
1AS.3   A young knight-errant: or, Cruising in the West
        Indies (161)
1AS.4   Strange sights abroad: or, A voyage in European
        waters (162)

Copyrighted: 1891-1893.
Publisher: Lee & Shepard; later Lothrop, Lee & Shepard.
Series Description: 'The bare announcement of a new series
    of books by Oliver Optic will delight boys all over the
    country. When they farther learn that their favorite
    author proposes to 'personally conduct' his army of
    readers on a grand tour of the world, there will be a
    terrible scramble for excursion tickets - that is, the
    opening volume of the 'Globe Trotting Series.' Of one
    thing the boys may be dead sure, it will be no tame, hum-
    drum journey, for Oliver Optic does not believe that fun
    and excitement are injurious to boys, but on the contrary,
    if of the right kind he thinks it does them good. Louis
    Belgrave is a fortunate lad, because, at the age of six-
    teen, he was the possessor of a cool million of dollars.
    No one, not even a young boy, can travel without money,
    as our author well knows, therefore he at once provided a
    liberal supply. Louis is a fine young fellow with good
    principles and honor, so he can be trusted to spend his
    million wisely. But he does not have entirely smooth

sailing. In the first place he has a rascally step-father
whom he had to subjugate, a dear mother to protect and
care for, and the missing million to find before he could
commence his delightful travels. They are all accomplished at last, and there was plenty of excitement and brave
exploits in the doing of them, as the boy readers will
find. The cover design shows many things - a globe, the
Eiffel tower, mountains, seas, rivers, castles and other
things Louis will see on his travels." Current Review.
[per L&S ad].

2AS ALL-OVER-THE-WORLD LIBRARY - Second series

2AS.1 American boys afloat: or, Cruising in the Orient
       (163)
2AS.2 The young navigators: or, The foreign cruise of the
       Maud (165)
2AS.3 Up and down the Nile: or, Young adventurers in Africa
       (166)
2AS.4 Asiatic breezes: or, Students on the wing (167)

Copyrighted: 1893-1894.
Publisher: Lee & Shepard; later Lothrop, Lee & Shepard.
Series Description: "The interest in these stories is
    continuous, and there is a great variety of exciting
    incident woven into the solid information which the book
    imparts so generously and without the slightest suspicion
    of dryness..." Boston Gazette. [per L&S ad].

3AS ALL-OVER-THE-WORLD LIBRARY - Third series

3AS.1 Across India: or, Live boys in the Far East (171)
3AS.2 Half round the world: or, Among the uncivilized (172)
3AS.3 Four young explorers: or, Sight-seeing in the tropics
       (176)
3AS.4 Pacific shores: or, Adventures in Eastern seas (177)

Copyrighted: 1895-1897.
Publisher: Lee & Shepard; later Lothrop, Lee & Shepard.
Series Description: "Amid such new and varied surroundings
    it would be surprising indeed if the author, with his
    faculty of making even the commonplace attractive, did
    not tell an intensely interesting story of adventure, as
    well as give much information in regard to the distant
    countries through which our friends pass, and the strange
    peoples with whom they are brought in contact...the whole
    series, is admirably adapted to reading aloud in the fam-
    ily circle, each volume containing matter which will
    interest all the members of the family." Boston Budget.
    [per L&S ad].

4AS   ARMY AND NAVY STORIES

4AS.1   The soldier boy: or, Tom Somers in the Army (36)
4AS.2   The sailor boy: or, Jack Somers in the Navy (37)
4AS.3   The young lieutenant: or, The adventures of an Army
             officer (42)
4AS.4   The Yankee middy: or, The adventures of a Naval
             officer (44)
4AS.5   Fighting Joe: or, The fortunes of a staff officer (46)
4AS.6   Brave Old Salt: or, Life on the quarter deck (48)

Copyrighted: 1863-1866.
Publisher: Lee & Shepard; later Lothrop, Lee & Shepard.
Series Description: "This series of six volumes recounts the
    adventures of two brothers, Tom and Jack Somers, one in
    the army, the other in the navy, in the great civil war.
    The romantic narratives of the fortunes and exploits of
    the brothers are thrilling in the extreme. Historical
    accuracy in the recital of the great events of that period
    is strictly followed, and the result is not only a library
    of entertaining volumes, but also the best history of the
    civil war for young people ever written." [per L&S ad].

    "The whole series are admirably illustrated from designs
    by Champney and Billings, printed and bound in the best
    style, and should be in the possession of any one who
    desires an interesting and graphic history of the prin-
    cipal events in the Great Rebellion." L&S ad in American
    Literary Gazette 5 (1 July 1865): 109.

Series Review: "...Mr. Adams... has written two army and
    two navy books, which are all spirited and correct enough,
    though seeming rather hasty in point of execution. It is
    unfortunate for the literary merit of children's books
    that there exists for them no high standard of criticism,
    and the temptations to a slovenly style are thus very
    strong..." North American Review 93 ns 102 (January
    1866): 242.

THE BLUE AND THE GRAY AFLOAT
    see THE BLUE AND THE GRAY SERIES

5AS   THE BLUE AND THE GRAY SERIES

5AS.1   Taken by the enemy (145)
5AS.2   Within the enemy's lines (149)
5AS.3   On the blocade (155)
5AS.4   Stand by the Union (157)
5AS.5   Fighting for the right (160)
5AS.6   A victorious Union (164)

Copyrighted: 1888-1893.

Publisher: Lee & Shepard; later Lothrop, Lee & Shepard.
Series Description: "The opening of a new series of books
    from the pen of Oliver Optic is bound to arouse the high-
    est anticipation in the minds of boy and girl readers.
    There never has been a more interesting writer in the
    field of juvenile literature than Mr. W.T. Adams, who,
    under his well-known pseudonym, is known and admired by
    every boy and girl in the country, and by thousands who
    have long since passed the boundaries of youth, yet who
    remember with pleasure the genial, interesting pen that
    did so much to interest, instruct and entertain their
    younger years...'The Blue and the Gray Series,' a title
    that is sufficiently indicative of the nature and spirit
    of the series...while the name of Oliver Optic is suffi-
    cient warrant of the absorbing style of narrative... A
    word, however, should be said in regard to the beauty and
    appropriateness of the binding, which makes it a most
    attractive volume." Boston Budget. [per L&S ad].

Also called The Blue and the Gray - Afloat.

Additional Information: The books of this series are bound
    in half blue, half gray cloth with lettering and emblem-
    atic dies in gilt. The medals read "Grand Army of the
    Republican Veteran 1861-1866" and "Confederate Veteran
    1861-1865."

"In the series of which this volume is the last, the
author has confined his narrative of adventures to the
navy. It has been suggested to him that another series,
[THE BLUE AND THE GRAY ON LAND] relating exclusively to
incidents in the army, should follow. After forty years
of labor in this particular field, and having already
exhausted the threescore and ten of human life, he cannot
be assured that he will live long enough to complete such
a series, though still in excellent health; but he intends
to make a beginning of the work as soon as other engage-
ments will permit." [Preface to A victorious Union].

6AS   THE BLUE AND THE GRAY ON LAND SERIES

6AS.1   Brother against brother: or, The war on the border
        (168)
6AS.2   In the saddle (170)
6AS.3   A lieutenant at eighteen (173)
6AS.4   On the staff (175)
6AS.5   At the front (178)
6AS.6   An undivided Union (179)

Copyrighted: 1894-1899.
Publisher: Lee & Shepard; later Lothrop, Lee & Shepard.
Series Description: "...This series is as bright and enter-
    taining as any work that Mr. Adams has yet put forth,
    and will be as eagerly perused as any that has borne his

name. It would not be fair to the prospective reader to
deprive him of the zest which comes from the unexpected
by entering into a synopsis of the story." Boston Budget.
[per L&S ad].

7AS BOAT-BUILDER SERIES

7AS.1 All adrift: or, The Goldwing Club (120)
7AS.2 Snug Harbor: or, The Champlain mechanics (125)
7AS.3 Square and compasses: or, Building the house (128)
7AS.4 Stem to stern: or, Building the boat (131)
7AS.5 All taut: or, Rigging the boat (133)
7AS.6 Ready about: or, Sailing the boat (138)

Copyrighted: 1882-1887.
Publisher: Lee & Shepard; later Lothrop, Lee & Shepard.
Series Description: "The series includes in six successive
    volumes the whole art of boat building, boat rigging,
    boat managing, and practical hints to make the ownership
    of a boat pay. A great deal of useful information is
    given in this Boat Builders Series, and in each book a
    very interesting story is interwoven with the information.
    Every reader will be interested at once in Dory, the hero
    of 'All Adrift,' and one of the characters retained in
    the subsequent volumes of the series. His friends will
    not want to lose sight of him, and every boy who makes
    his acquaintance in 'All Adrift' will become his friend."
    [L&S ad].

8AS BOAT CLUB SERIES

8AS.1 The boat club: or, The Bunkers of Rippleton (3)
8AS.2 All aboard: or, Life on the lake (4)
8AS.3 Now or never: or, The adventures of Bobby Bright (5)
8AS.4 Try again: or, The trials and triumphs of Harry West
       (6)
8AS.5 Poor and proud: or, The fortunes of Katy Redburn (9)
8AS.6 Little by little: or, The cruise of the Flyaway (15)

Copyrighted: 1854-1360.
Publisher: Brown, Bazin and Co., vol. 1-3
            Brown, Taggard and Chase, vol. 4
            Phillips, Sampson and Co., vol. 5
            Crosby, Nichols, Lee Co., vol. 6
            Lee & Shepard; later Lothrop, Lee &
              Shepard, vol. 1-6
Series Description: "This is the first series of books
    written for the young by 'Oliver Optic.' It laid the
    foundation for his fame as the first of authors in which
    the young delight, and gained for him the title of the
    Prince of Story-Tellers. The six books are varied in
    incident and plot, but all are entertaining and original."
    [L&S ad].

"The six volumes comprising the 'Oliver Optic Series' are among the most deservedly popular juveniles ever issued. Attractive in style, and peculiarly interesting in the narrative, they invariably secure the attention of the reader, and at the same time inculcate the most wholesome moral principles." American Literary Gazette 8 (1 December 1862): 135.

Series Review: "...The 'Boat Club' books are the best; they are fresh and lively, with a good deal of boyish slang, and a great deal of adventure. Neither of these traits is a serious objection; but the critic-pen must demur when a well-taught school-girl is made to say, 'I don't know as you will,'... But these are trifles; and this writer's books, though evidently written with a rapidity that seems to take one's breath away, are certainly effective, and must be popular." North American Review 93 ns v.102 (January 1866): 248.

Additional Information: The first three titles were originally published by Brown, Bazin & Co. Try Again was issued under the imprint of Brown, Taggard & Chase until their collapse in 1857. Phillips, Sampson and Co. received the copyright for Poor and Proud in late 1858 and took over publication of the preceding four titles until 1859, when they went out of business. William Lee reprinted the five existing titles in the Fall of 1860, as well as originally publishing Little By Little under the imprint of Crosby, Nichols, Lee and Co. These titles were dropped when he left the firm in 1861. The whole series was reissued by Lee & Shepard in 1862. [Cf. Kilgour. Lee & Shepard: publishers of the people, p.34].

When first published by Lee & Shepard in 1862, the "series was uniformly bound in reddish-brown cloth, with gilded title and designs on the spine...with a highly pictorial title page, on which the title, author and imprint are in rustic letters and a facing frontispiece, the only separate illustration in the book... The books were printed by Rand and Avery" with illustrations by Hammatt Billings. [Cf. Kilgour. Lee & Shepard: publishers of the people, p. 28].

When Lee & Shepard first advertised the series (American Literary Gazette 1 December 1862: 135), they entitled it 'Oliver Optic Series'. In another ad (American Literary Gazette 15 September 1864: 315), the six titles were listed for sale as the 'Library for Young People' in a boxed set. The same books were later advertised as the 'Famous "Boat-Club" Series, A Library for Young People.' Finally, the more familiar title, 'Boat Club Series' was used.

9AS   FLORA LEE STORY BOOKS

9AS.1   The picnic party (27)
9AS.2   The gold thimble (28)
9AS.3   The do-somethings (29)
9AS.4   The Christmas gift (20)
9AS.5   Uncle Ben (22)
9AS.6   The birthday party (23)

Publisher: Lee & Shepard.
Series Description: see RIVERDALE STORIES (12AS).
Other Information: These six titles were originally issued
    as part of the RIVERDALE STORIES (12AS). The remaining
    six titles of the RIVERDALE STORIES were reissued under
    the series title RIVERDALE STORY BOOKS (13AS). The
    numbered order of the titles varies. This series was
    advertised in the American Literary Gazette 3 (15
    September 1864): 315. It was also called the FLORA LEE
    LIBRARY.

10AS   GREAT WESTERN SERIES

10AS.1   Going west: or, The perils of a poor boy (98)
10AS.2   Out west: or, Roughing it on the Great Lakes (103)
10AS.3   Lake breezes: or, The cruise of the Sylvania (107)
10AS.4   Going south: or, Yachting on the Atlantic coast (109)
10AS.5   Down south: or, Yacht adventures in Florida (111)
10AS.6   Up the river: or, Yachting on the Mississippi (114)

Copyrighted: 1875-1881.
Publisher: Lee & Shepard; later Lothrop, Lee & Shepard.
Series Description: "This is the latest series of books
    issued by this popular writer, and dealt with life on
    the Great Lakes, for which a careful study was made by
    the author in a summer tour of the immense water sources
    of America. The story, which carries the same hero
    through the six books of the series, is always entertain-
    ing, novel scenes and varied incidents giving a constantly
    changing yet always attractive aspect to the narrative.
    Oliver Optic has written nothing better." [L&S ad].

Other Information: Going West was serialized in Oliver
    Optic's Magazine (13S.26) before being published as a
    full length book.

11AS   LAKE SHORE SERIES

11AS.1   Through by daylight: or, The young engineer of the
            Lake Shore Railroad (66)
11AS.2   Lightning Express: or, The rival academies (68)
11AS.3   On time: or, The young captain of the Ucayga
            steamer (69)
11AS.4   Switch off: or, The war of the students (70)
11AS.5   Brake up: or, The young peacemakers (71)

11AS.6   Bear and forbear: or, The young skipper of Lake
         Ucayga (74)

Copyrighted: 1869-1870.
Publisher: Lee & Shepard; later Lothrop, Lee & Shepard.
Series Description: "...six stories, whose locality and
    principal characters are nearly the same...The railroad,
    which is the basis of the incidents in the first and
    second volumes, was suggested by the experience of several
    young gentlemen in Ohio, who had formed a company, and
    transacted all the business of a railroad in regular form,
    for the purpose of obtaining a practical knowledge of the
    details of such a corporation...The young engineer is
    doubtless a smart boy...If he has an 'old head,' he has a
    young heart, which he endeavors to keep pure and true. As
    he appears in this and the subsequent volumes of the
    series, the author is willing to commend him as an example
    of the moral and Christian hero, who cannot lead his
    imitators astray; for he loves truth and goodness, and is
    willing to forgive and serve his enemies." [preface of
    Through by Daylight].

Other Information: The titles in this series were serialized
    in Oliver Optic's Magazine (13S.8-13S.13) before they were
    published as full length books.

ONWARD AND UPWARD SERIES
    see UPWARD AND ONWARD SERIES

12AS   RIVERDALE STORIES

12AS.1   The little merchant (18)
12AS.2   The young voyagers (19)
12AS.3   The Christmas gift (20)
12AS.4   Dolly and I (21)
12AS.5   Uncle Ben (22)
12AS.6   The birthday party (23)
12AS.7   Proud and lazy (24)
12AS.8   Careless Kate (25)
12AS.9   Robinson Crusoe, Jr. (26)
12AS.10 The picnic party (27)
12AS.11 The gold thimble (28)
12AS.12 The do-somethings (29)

Copyrighted: 1862.
Publisher: Lee & Shepard; later Lothrop, Lee & Shepard.
Series Description: "The 'RIVERDALE STORIES' are a series of
    short bright stories for younger children than those who
    are able to comprehend 'The STARRY FLAG SERIES,' 'The
    WOODVILLE STORIES,' 'ARMY AND NAVY STORIES,' &c. But they
    all display the author's talent for pleasing 'Little Folks'
    as well as the older children. They are all fresh, taking

stories, preaching no sermons but inculcating good lessons."
[L&S ad].

Series Review: "These books are intended for children from
    six to ten years of age, and while they are admirably
    adapted to the understanding of such, they teach healthy
    moral lessons without being dull and spiritless. They are
    stories of live children, and fit for live children to
    read. Each volume contains a separate story; and the
    books are beautifully printed and bound, and illustrated
    in the highest style of art." American Literary Gazette
    8 (1 December 1862): 135.

    "...The dozen little 'RIVERDALE' specimens are in very
    large type, for very little children..." North American
    Review 93 ns 102 (January 1866): 248.

Other Information: These twelve titles are split into two
    groups of six and are also issued under the series titles
    of FLORA LEE STORY BOOKS (9AS) and RIVERDALE STORY BOOKS
    (13AS). The two series were advertised in American
    Literary Gazette 3 (15 September 1864): 315.

13AS   RIVERDALE STORY BOOKS

13AS.1   The little merchant (18)
13AS.2   The young voyagers (19)
13AS.3   Dolly and I (21)
13AS.4   Proud and lazy (24)
13AS.5   Careless Kate (25)
13AS.6   Robinson Crusoe, Jr. (26)

Publisher: Lee & Shepard.
Series Description: See RIVERDALE STORIES (12AS).
Other Information: These six titles were originally issued
    as part of the RIVERDALE STORIES (12AS). The remaining
    six titles of the RIVERDALE STORIES were re-issued under
    the series title FLORA LEE STORY BOOKS (9AS). The number-
    ed order of the titles varies. This series was advertised
    in American Literary Gazette 3 (15 September 1864): 315.

14AS   SAILOR BOY SERIES

14AS.1   The sailor boy: or, Jack Somers in the Navy (37)
14AS.2   The Yankee middy: or, The adventures of a naval
             officer (44)
14AS.3   Brave Old Salt: or, Life on the quarter deck (48)

Publisher: Lee & Shepard; later Lothrop, Lee & Shepard.
Series Description: see ARMY AND NAVY STORIES (4AS).
Other Information: These three titles were originally issued
    as v.2, 4, and 6 of the ARMY AND NAVY STORIES (4AS). Vol-

umes 1, 3, and 5 of the ARMY AND NAVY STORIES were re-
issued as the SOLDIER BOY SERIES (15AS).

15AS   SOLDIER BOY SERIES

15AS.1   The soldier boy: or, Tom Somers in the Army (36)
15AS.2   The young lieutenant: or, The adventures of an Army
         officer (42)
15AS.3   Fighting Joe: or, The fortunes of a staff officer (46)

Publisher: Lee & Shepard; later Lothrop, Lee & Shepard.
Series Description: see ARMY AND NAVY STORIES (4AS).
Other Information: These three titles were originally issued
   as v. 1, 3, and 5 of the ARMY AND NAVY STORIES (4AS).
   Volumes 2, 4, and 6 were re-issued as the SAILOR BOY
   SERIES (14AS).

16AS   STARRY FLAG SERIES

16AS.1   The starry flag: or, The young fisherman of Cape Ann
         (55)
16AS.2   Breaking away: or, The fortunes of a student (56)
16AS.3   Seek and find: or, The adventures of a smart boy (58)
16AS.4   Freaks of fortune: or, Half round the world (61)
16AS.5   Make or break: or, The rich man's daughter (62)
16AS.6   Down the river: or, Buck Bradford and his tyrants (64)

Copyrighted: 1867-1868.
Publisher: Lee & Shepard; later Lothrop, Lee & Shepard.
Series Description: "These books are exciting narratives, and
   full of stirring adventures, but the youthful heroes of
   the stories are noble, self-sacrificing, and courageous,
   and the stories contain nothing which will do injury to
   the mind or heart of the youthful reader." Webster Times.
   [per L&S ad].

   "...Since the publication of 'The Starry Flag' was completed in the Magazine, the author has found allusions to
   it in at least a hundred letters from young persons, who
   seem to be strongly impressed with the opinion that the
   whole story has not been told. Though it was not his
   original purpose to write a second story with the same
   characters, the author has neither the inclination nor
   the courage to disappoint his young friends, and at no
   distant period the fortunes of Levi Fairfield and Bessie
   Watson will be followed to a more satisfactory conclusion
   in a sequel to The Starry Flag." [preface to The Starry
   Flag].

   The titles in this series were serialized in Oliver Optic's
   Magazine before being published as full length books.

17AS   UPWARD AND ONWARD SERIES

17AS.1   Field and forest: or, The fortunes of a farmer (75)
17AS.2   Plane and plank: or, The mishaps of a mechanic (76)
17AS.3   Desk and debit: or, The catastrophes of a clerk (77)
17AS.4   Cringle and cross-tree: or, The sea swashes of a
           sailor (79)
17AS.5   Bivouac and battle: or, The struggles of a soldier
           (81)
17AS.6   Sea and shore: or, The tramps of a traveller (82)

Copyrighted: 1870-1872.
Publisher: Lee & Shepard; later Lothrop, Lee & Shepard.
Series Description: "Paul Farringford, the hero of these
    tales, is, like most of this author's heroes, a young man
    of high spirit, and of high aims and correct principles,
    appearing in the different volumes as a farmer, a captain,
    a bookkeeper, a soldier, a sailor, and a traveller. In
    all of them the hero meets with very exciting adventures,
    told in the graphic style for which the author is famous."
    [L&S ad].

Other Information: The titles in this series were serialized
    in Oliver Optic's Magazine (13S.14-13S.19) before being
    published as full length books.

18AS   WOODVILLE STORIES

18AS.1   Rich and humble: or, The mission of Bertha Grant (34)
18AS.2   In school and out: or, The conquest of Richard Grant
           (35)
18AS.3   Watch and wait: or, The young fugitives (40)
18AS.4   Work and win: or, Noddy Newman on a cruise (45)
18AS.5   Hope and have: or, Fanny Grant among the Indians (49)
18AS.6   Haste and waste: or, The young pilot of Lake Champlain
           (50)

Copyrighted: 1863-1866.
Publisher: Lee & Shepard; later Lothrop, Lee & Shepard.
Series Review: "Though we are not so young as we once
    were, we relished these stories almost as much as the boys
    and girls for whom they were written. They were really
    refreshing, even to us. There is much in them which is
    calculated to inspire a generous, healthy ambition, and
    to make distasteful all reading tending to stimulate base
    desires." Fitchburg Reveille. [per L&S ad].

"Oliver Optic is the apostolic successor, at the 'Hub' of
    Peter Parley...The best notice to give of them [Woodville
    Stories] is to mention that a couple of youngsters pulled
    them out of a pile two hours since, and are yet devouring
    them out in the summer-house...oblivious to muffin time."
    N.Y. Leader. [per L&S ad].

19AS   YACHT CLUB SERIES

19AS.1   Little Bobtail: or, The wreck of the Penobscot (84)
19AS.2   The yacht club: or, The young boat-builder (87)
19AS.3   Money-maker: or, The victory of the Basilisk (89)
19AS.4   The coming wave: or, The hidden treasure of High
         Rock (91)
19AS.5   The Dorcas Club: or, Our girls afloat (92)
19AS.6   Ocean-born: or, The cruise of the clubs (96)

Copyrighted: 1872-1875.
Publisher: Lee & Shepard; later Lothrop, Lee & Shepard.
Series Review: "The series has this peculiarity, that
    all of its constituent volumes are independent of one
    another, and therefore each story is complete in itself.
    'Oliver Optic' is perhaps the favorite author of the boys
    and girls of this country, and he seems destined to enjoy
    an endless popularity. He deserves his success, for he
    makes very interesting stories, and inculcates none but
    the best sentiments; and the 'Yacht Club' is no exception
    to this rule." New Haven Journal and Courier.
    [per L&S ad].

Other Information: The titles in this series were serialized
    in Oliver Optic's Magazine (13S.20-13S.25) before being
    published as full length books.

20AS   YOUNG AMERICA ABROAD: A Library of Travel and Adventure
       in Foreign Lands   First Series

20AS.1   Outward bound: or, Young America afloat (51)
20AS.2   Shamrock and thistle: or, Young America in Ireland
         and Scotland (59)
20AS.3   Red cross: or, Young America in England and Wales (60)
20AS.4   Dikes and ditches: or, Young America in Holland and
         Belgium (63)
20AS.5   Palace and cottage: or, Young America in France and
         Switzerland (67)
20AS.6   Down the Rhine: or, Young America in Germany (72)

Copyrighted: 1866-1869.
Publisher: Lee & Shepard; later Lothrop, Lee & Shepard.
Series Description: "The publishers take pleasure in
    announcing to the trade a new series of juveniles by
    the very popular author, William Taylor Adams, Esq.
    (Oliver Optic)." American Literary Gazette 8 (1 November
    1866): 36.

Series Review: "The story from its inception and through
    the twelve volumes (see second series), is a bewitching
    one, while the information imparted, concerning the coun-
    tries of Europe and the isles of the sea, is not only
    correct in every particular, but is told in a captivating
    style.   'Oliver Optic' will continue to be the boy's

friend, and his pleasant books will continue to be read by thousands of American boys. What a fine holiday present either or both series of 'Young America Abroad' would be for a young friend!..." Providence Press. [per L&S ad].

"These are by far the most instructive books written by this popular author, and while maintaining throughout enough of excitement and adventure to enchain the interest of the youthful reader, there is still a great amount of information conveyed respecting the history, natural features, and geography of this far-off land, and the peculiarities of the places and people which they contain." Gazette. [per L&S ad].

"...The author expresses the hope that the volumes of the series will not only be instructive as a description of foreign lands, and interesting as a record of juvenile exploits, but that they will convey correct views of moral and social duties, and stimulate the young reader to their faithful performance. The series will be unlike the other many books from the pen of this favorite author, if they do not answer this description." Hours at Home 6 (April 1868): 571.

Other Information: These titles were not serialized in Oliver Optic's Magazine.

21AS YOUNG AMERICA ABROAD: A Library of Travel and Adventure
      in Foreign Lands   Second Series

21AS.1 Up the Baltic: or, Young America in Norway, Sweden,
        and Denmark (80)
21AS.2 Northern lands: or, Young America in Russia and
        Prussia (83)
21AS.3 Cross and crescent: or, Young America in Turkey and
        Greece (85)
21AS.4 Sunny shores: or, Young America in Italy and Austria
        (93)
21AS.5 Vine and olive: or, Young America in Spain and
        Portugal (102)
21AS.6 Isles of the sea: or, Young America homeward bound
        (106)

Copyrighted: 1871-1877.
Publisher: Lee & Shepard; later Lothrop, Lee & Shepard.
Series Description: "Young America, Ahoy! 100,000 boys and
    girls who accompanied the academy ship, Young America
    abroad, as recorded in the first series of Log Books
    under the titles... are hereby notified that the 'Young
    America' refitted and provisioned by her old commander,
    is again afloat and continuing her voyages abroad. The
    account of her trip and the adventures of her crew will
    be given to Our Boys and Girls, under the title of Up
    the Baltic...ready at the bookstores all over the country,

Saturday June 17 [1871]." American Literary Gazette 17
(15 June 1871): 107.

Series Review: "'Oliver Optic' is a nom de plume that is
known and loved by almost every boy of intelligence in
the land. We have seen a highly intellectual and world-
weary man, a cynic whose heart was somewhat imbittered
by its large experience of human nature, take up one of
Oliver Optic's books and read it at a sitting, neglecting
his work in yielding to the fascination of the pages.
When a mature and exceedingly well-informed mind, long
despoiled of all its freshness, can thus find pleasure
in a book for boys, no additional words of recommendation
are needed." Sunday Times. [per L&S ad].

Also reviewed in Harper's 43 (September 1871): 624.

Other Information: These titles were not serialized in
Oliver Optic's Magazine.

PUBLISHER SERIES

The number in parenthesis following the title refers to the
CHRONOLOGICAL LIST entry number. The number directly preceding the title refers to the original number in the publisher
series. The titles are listed in the order determined by
the publisher series numbering. If the series was not number-
ed by the publisher, the titles are arranged alphabetically.
For example, Among the missing is #124 of the Alger Series,
published January 1925. It is #153 in the CHRONOLOGICAL LIST
and 2PS.1 in the PUBLISHER SERIES.

1PS ADVENTURE AND JUNGLE SERIES (Donohue)

1PS.1 #2 Casket of diamonds, The (142)

2PS ALGER SERIES (Street & Smith)

Series Description: "There are legions of boys of foreign
    parents who are being helped along the road to true
    Americanism by reading these books which are so peculiar-
    ly American in tone that the reader cannot fail to absorb
    some of the spirit of fair play and clean living which is
    so characteristically American. In this list will be
    included certain books by Edward Stratemeyer, Oliver
    Optic, and other authors who wrote the Alger type of
    stories, which are equal in interest and wholesomeness
    with those written by the famous author after which this
    great line of books for boys is named." [Street & Smith
    ad].

2PS.1   #124 Among the missing (153) January 1925
2PS.2   #125 His own helper (132) January 1925
2PS.3   #126 Honest Kit Dunstable (186) February 1925
2PS.4   #127 Every inch a boy (127) February 1925
2PS.5   #128 Young pilot, The (187) March 1925
2PS.6   #129 Always in luck (135) March 1925

```
2PS.7    #130  Rich and humble (34) March 1925
2PS.8    #131  In school and out (35) April 1925
2PS.9    #132  Watch and wait (40) April 1925
2PS.10   #133  Work and win (45) May 1925
2PS.11   #134  Hope and have (49) May 1925
2PS.12   #135  Haste and waste (50) June 1925
2PS.13   #136  Royal Tarr's pluck (184) June 1925
2PS.14   #137  Prisoners of the cave, The (147)
2PS.15   #138  Louis Chiswick's mission (182)
2PS.16   #139  Professor's son, The (126)
2PS.17   #140  Young hermit, The (144)
2PS.18   #141  Cruise of "The Dandy", The (141)
2PS.19   #142  Building himself up (115)
2PS.20   #143  Lyon Hart's heroism (183)
2PS.21   #144  Three young silver kings (137)
2PS.22   #145  Making a man of himself (124)
2PS.23   #146  Striving for his own (185)
2PS.24   #147  Through by daylight (66)
2PS.25   #148  Lightning Express (68)
2PS.26   #149  On time (69)
2PS.27   #150  Switch off (70)
2PS.28   #151  Brake up (71) January 1926
2PS.29   #152  Bear and forbear (74) January 1926
2PS.30   #153  Starry flag, The (55) February 1926
2PS.31   #154  Breaking away (56) February 1926
2PS.32   #155  Seek and find (58)  March 1926
2PS.33   #156  Freaks of fortune (61) March 1926
2PS.34   #157  Make or break (62) April 1926
2PS.35   #158  Down the river (64) April 1926
2PS.36   #159  Boat club, The (3)  May 1926
2PS.37   #160  All aboard  (4) May 1926
2PS.38   #161  Now or never (5) June 1926
2PS.39   #162  Try again (6) June 1926
2PS.40   #163  Poor and proud (9) July 1926
2PS.41   #164  Little by little (15) July 1926
2PS.42   #165  Sailor boy, The (37) July 1926
2PS.43   #166  Yankee middy, The (44) August 1926
2PS.44   #167  Brave Old Salt (48) August 1926
```

```
3PS  AMERICAN BOYS' SERIES  (Lee & Shepard;
       Lothrop, Lee & Shepard)
       Note:  Lee & Shepard published only #2-65.
```

```
3PS.1    #2   All aboard (4)
3PS.2    #5   Boat club, The (3)
3PS.3    #21  Haste or waste (50)
3PS.4    #22  Hope and have (49)
3PS.5    #23  In school and out (35)
3PS.6    #25  Just his luck (105)
3PS.7    #27  Little by little (15)
3PS.8    #31  Now or never (5)
3PS.9    #32  Poor and proud (9)
3PS.10   #33  Rich and humble (34)
3PS.11   #40  Try again (6)
```

```
3PS.12   #43   Watch and wait (40)
3PS.13   #47   Work and win (45)
3PS.14   #51   Field and forest (75)
3PS.15   #52   Outward bound (51)
3PS.16   #53   Soldier boy, The (36)
3PS.17   #54   Starry flag, The (55)
3PS.18   #55   Through by daylight (66)
3PS.19   #62   Missing million, A (158)
3PS.20   #63   Millionaire at sixteen, A (159)
3PS.21   #64   Young knight-errant, A (161)
3PS.22   #65   Strange sights abroad (162)
3PS.23   #89   Going west (98)
3PS.24   #90   Little Bobtail (84)
3PS.25   #95   All adrift (120)
3PS.26   #100  Up the Baltic (80)
```

4PS   ARGYLE SERIES   (Hurst)

4PS.1   Little by little (15)

5PS   BERKELEY SERIES   (American Publishers)

5PS.1   Casket of diamonds, The (142)

6PS   BEST BOOKS FOR BOYS   (Caldwell)

```
6PS.1   #4    All aboard (4)
6PS.2   #8    Boat club, The (3)
6PS.3   #36   Now or never (5)
```

7PS   BLACK HERITAGE LIBRARY COLLECTION
        (Books for Libraries Press)

7PS.1   Hatchie, the guardian slave (1)

8PS   BOAT CLUB SERIES   (Caldwell)

```
8PS.1   All aboard (4)
8PS.2   Boat club, The (3)
8PS.3   Little by little (15)
8PS.4   Now or never (5)
8PS.5   Poor and proud (9)
8PS.6   Try again (6)
```

9PS   BOAT CLUB SERIES (Henneberry)

9PS.1   All aboard (4)
9PS.2   Boat club, The (3)
9PS.3   Little by little (15)
9PS.4   Now or never (5)
9PS.5   Poor and proud (9)
9PS.6   Try again (6)

10PS   BOAT CLUB SERIES (Mershon)

10PS.1   All aboard (4)
10PS.2   Boat club, The (3)
10PS.3   Little by little (15)
10PS.4   Now or never (5)
10PS.5   Poor and proud (9)
10PS.6   Try again (6)

11PS   BOUND TO WIN SERIES (Donohue)

11PS.1   #8   All aboard (4)
11PS.2   #11   Boat club, The (3)
11PS.3   #53   Little by little (15)
11PS.4   #59   Now or never (5)
11PS.5   #67   Poor and proud (9)
11PS.6   #88   Try again (6)

12PS   BOYS BANNER SERIES (Donohue)

Series Description: A desirable assortment of books for
    boys, by standard and favorite authors. Each title
    is complete and unabridged. Printed on a good quality
    of paper from large, clear type. Beautifully bound in
    cloth. Each book is wrapped in a special multi-colored
    jacket. [Donohue ad].

12PS.1   #4   In school and out (35)
12PS.2   #9   Little by little (15)
12PS.3   #11   Now or never (5)

13PS   BOY'S LIBERTY SERIES   (Donohue)

13PS.1   #8   Little by little (15)
13PS.2   #12   Poor and proud (9)
13PS.3   #18   Try again (6)

14PS   THE BOYS' OWN LIBRARY   (Federal Book Co.)

Series Description: Brooks McCormick: Four splendid books
     of adventure on sea and land, by this well-known English
     writer for boys. Originally published about fifteen
     years ago, these books are in steady demand today.
     [Federal ad].

14PS.1   Giant islanders, The (146)
14PS.2   How he won (139)
14PS.3   Nature's young noblemen (136)
14PS.4   Rival battalions, The (148)

Series Description: William Taylor Adams (Oliver Optic) has
     devoted a lifetime to writing literature for young people
     and requires no introduction to the reading public. Of
     the hundred or more stories from his pen, we offer six of
     the best. [Federal ad].

14PS.5   All aboard (4)
14PS.6   Boat club, The (3)
14PS.7   Little by little (15)
14PS.8   Now or never (5)
14PS.9   Poor and proud (9)
14PS.10   Try again (6)

Series Description: Gayle Winterton: This very interesting
     story relates the trials and triumphs of a young Amer-
     ican actor, including the solution of a very puzzling
     mystery. [Federal ad].

14PS.11 Young actor, The (152)

15PS   THE BOYS' OWN LIBRARY   (McKay)

Series Description: Brooks McCormick: Four splendid books of
     adventure on sea and land, by this well-known writer for
     boys. [McKay ad].

15PS.1   Giant islanders, The (146)
15PS.2   How he won (139)
15PS.3   Nature's young nobleman (136)
15PS.4   Rival battalions, The (148)

Series Description: Gayle Winterton: This very interesting
     story relates the trials and triumphs of a Young American
     actor, including the solution of a very puzzling mystery.
     [McKay ad].

15PS.5 Young actor, The (152)

16PS   BOYS' OWN LIBRARY   (Street & Smith)

Series Description: The titles in this splendid juvenile
    series have been selected with care, and as a result all
    the stories can be relied upon for their excellence.
    They are bright and sparkling, not overburdened with
    lengthy descriptions, but brimful of adventure from the
    first page to the last - in fact, they are just the kind
    of yarns that appeal strongly to the healthy boy who is
    fond of thrilling exploits and deeds of heroism. Among
    the authors whose names are included...are Horatio Alger,
    Jr., Edward S. Ellis, James Otis, Arthur M. Winfield
    and Frank H. Converse. In cloth. Attractive covers.
    [Street & Smith ad].

16PS.1   #47   Giant islanders, The by Brooks McCormick (146)
16PS.2   #57   How he won by Brooks McCormick (139)
16PS.3   #78   Nature's young nobleman by Brooks McCormick
                (136)
16PS.4   #93   Rival battalions, The by Brooks McCormick (148)
16PS.5   #127   Young actor, The by Gayle Winterton (152)

17PS BOYS' POPULAR LIBRARY (Street & Smith; McKay; Federal)

Series Description: An excellent series of books for boys by
    such popular authors as Optic, Kingston and other well-
    known writers. These books are bound in cloth, with very
    attractive cover designs stamped in colors. They are
    well printed from large type, on good paper. Printed
    wrappers. [Federal ad].

17PS.1   #1   All aboard (4)
17PS.2   #3   Boat club, The (3)
17PS.3   #24   Little by little (15)
17PS.4   #31   Now or never (5)
17PS.5   #45   Try again (6)

18PS   CAMBRIDGE CLASSICS   (Hurst)

18PS.1   In school and out (35)
18PS.2   Little by little (15)
18PS.3   Rich and humble (34)

19PS   EMPIRE EDITION   (American News)

19PS.1   Now or never (5)
19PS.2   Try again (6)
19PS.3   All aboard (4)
19PS.4   Boat club, The (3)

20PS   EMPIRE EDITION   (New York Publishing Co.)

20PS.1 Poor and proud (9)

21PS   FAMOUS ADVENTURE SERIES   (McKay)

21PS.1 #5 How he won by Brooks McCormick (139)

22PS   FAMOUS BOOKS FOR BOYS   (Caldwell)

22PS.1 #1 All aboard (4)
22PS.2 #3 Boat club, The (3)

23PS   FIRESIDE HENTY SERIES   (Donohue)

23PS.1 Boat club, The (3)

24PS   FIRESIDE SERIES   (Hurst)

24PS.1 Oliver Optic's new story book (180)

25PS   GENEVA BOOK   (Carlton Press)

25PS.1 Boat club, The (3)

26PS   GILT TOP SERIES   (Hurst)

26PS.1 Little by little (15)

27PS   THE GOLD SERIES   (F.M. Lupton)

27PS.1 All aboard (4)
27PS.2 Boat club, The (3)

28PS   GOOD COMPANY SERIES   (Lee & Shepard)

28PS.1 #3 Three millions! or, The way of the world (53)

29PS   HAPPY THOUGHT SERIES   (Street & Smith)

29PS.1   #5   Young pilot, The (187)

30PS   HEARTHSTONE SERIES   (Lee & Shepard)

30PS.1   v.4   Getting an indorser and other stories (95)

31PS   HOME SERIES FOR GIRLS   (Hurst)

31PS.1   Do-somethings, The (29) October 14, 1905
31PS.2   Proud and lazy (24) September 16, 1905

32PS   THE HOUSEHOLD LIBRARY   (Lee & Shepard)

32PS.1   v.1   In doors and out: or, Views from the
                    chimney corner (2)
32PS.2   v.2   Living too fast (101)
32PS.3   v.3   Way of the world, The (52)

33PS   LAURELHURST SERIES   (Hurst)

33PS.1   In school and out (35)
33PS.2   Little by little (15)
33PS.3   Rich and humble (34)

34PS   LEATHERCLAD TALES   (Lovell)

34PS.1   #6   Nature's young noblemen (136)

35PS   LEATHERCLAD TALES   (United States Book Co.)

35PS.1   #27   Young actor, The (152)
35PS.2   #29   Rival battalions, The (148)

36PS   LIBRARY FOR YOUNG PEOPLE   (Hurst)

36PS.1   #6   Little by little (15)

37PS   LIBRARY FOR YOUNG PEOPLE   (Rickey, Mallory)

37PS.1 All aboard (4)
37PS.2 Boat club, The (3)
37PS.3 Little by little (15)
37PS.4 Now or never (5)
37PS.5 Poor and proud (9)
37PS.6 Try again (6)

38PS LOG CABIN LIBRARY - LOG CABIN SERIES
        (Log Cabin Press)

38PS.1 #16 Outward bound (51)

39PS LUCKY SERIES (George Munro's Sons)

39PS.1 Boat club, The (3)

40PS "LUPTON" GILT TOP (Federal; formerly F.M. Lupton)

Series description: These books are printed from large type
    plates on a fine quality of book paper and are bound in
    an extra finished cloth. Titles stamped in gold. Inset
    frontispieces. The list consists of 248 selected
    titles...including a number of exclusive copyright books.
    No other line of Gilt Top 12mos. published at less than
    $1.00, equals this series. Printed wrappers. [Federal
    ad].

40PS.1 All aboard (4)
40PS.2 Boat club, The (3)
40PS.3 Now or never (5)
40PS.4 Poor and proud (9)
40PS.5 Try again (6)

41PS THE MACLELLAN BOOKS (MacLellan)

41PS.1 Outward bound (51)

42PS MEDAL LIBRARY (Street & Smith)

Series description: This is an ideal line for boys of all
    ages. It contains juvenile masterpieces by the most
    popular writers of interesting fiction for boys... the
    best works of Oliver Optic, another author whose entire
    life was devoted to writing books that would tend to in-
    terest and elevate our boys. [Street & Smith ad].

Additional information: "The Medal Library was a paperback
    reprint series published from January 28, 1899 to Septem-
    ber 24, 1906, for a total of 378 issues. [Eighteen were
    written by Adams]. All except the first eight were issued
    weekly. On October 1, 1906, the series was retitled and
    no. 379 appeared as the New Medal Library (44PS)."
    [Cf. Johnson. Stratemeyer pseudonyms and series books,
    p. 54].

42PS.1   #1   Boat club, The (3)
42PS.2   #3   All aboard (4)
42PS.3   #5   Now or never (5)
42PS.4   #9   Try again (6)
42PS.5   #46   Poor and proud (9)
42PS.6   #56   Nature's young nobleman (136)
                    (by Brooks McCormick)
42PS.7   #62   How he won (139)
                    (by Brooks McCormick)
42PS.8   #79   Rival battalions, The (148)
                    (by Brooks McCormick)
42PS.9   #97   Giant islanders, The (146)
                    (by Brooks McCormick)
42PS.10   #105   Young actor, The (152)
                    (by Gayle Winterton)
42PS.11   #160   Little by little (15)
42PS.12   #174   Haste and waste (50)
42PS.13   #179   Hope and have (49)
42PS.14   #311   Work and win (45)
42PS.15   #315   Watch and wait (40)
42PS.16   #333   Rich and humble (34)
42PS.17   #339   In school and out (35)
42PS.18   #375   Sailor boy, The (37)

43PS MUNSEY'S POPULAR SERIES (F.A. Munsey)

43PS.1   #14   Nature's young nobleman (136)

44PS NEW MEDAL LIBRARY (Street & Smith)

Additional information: "On October 1, 1906, the
    series [Medal Library (42PS)] was retitled and
    no. 379 appeared as the New Medal Library. The
    New Medal Library continued until December 7,
    1915, and ended with no. 858." [Cf. Johnson.
    Stratemeyer pseudonyms and series books, p. 54].

44PS.1   #382   Yankee middy, The (44)
44PS.2   #387   Brave Old Salt (48)
44PS.3   #393   Starry flag, The (55)
44PS.4   #397   Breaking away (56)
44PS.5   #405   Seek and find (58)
44PS.6   #412   Freaks of fortune (61)

```
44PS.7    #418   Make or break (62)
44PS.8    #424   Down the river (64)
44PS.9    #430   Through by daylight (66)
44PS.10   #435   Lightning Express (68)
44PS.11   #441   On time (69)
44PS.12   #447   Switch off (70)
44PS.13   #453   Brake up (71)
44PS.14   #460   Bear and forbear (74)
44PS.15   #523   Building himself up (115)
44PS.16   #528   Lyon Hart's heroism (183)
44PS.17   #534   Louis Chiswick's mission (182)
44PS.18   #540   Royal Tarr's pluck (184)
44PS.19   #546   Professor's son, The (126)
44PS.20   #552   Striving for his own (185)
44PS.21   #559   Making a man of himself (124)
44PS.22   #565   Every inch a boy (127)
44PS.23   #571   His own helper (132)
44PS.24   #577   Honest Kit Dunstable (186)
44PS.25   #583   Young pilot, The (187)
44PS.26   #589   Cruise of the "Dandy", The (141)
44PS.27   #595   Three young silver kings (137)
44PS.28   #603   Young hermit of Lake Minnetonka, The (144)
44PS.29   #615   Prisoners of the cave, The (147)
44PS.30   #627   Among the missing (153)
44PS.31   #634   Always in luck (135)
```

45PS   OLIVER OPTIC BOOKS   (Hurst)

Series Description: Few boys are alive to-day who have not
   read some of the writings of this famous author, whose
   books are scattered broadcast and eagerly sought for.
   Oliver Optic has the faculty of writing books full of
   dash and energy, such as healthy boys want and need.

```
45PS.1    All aboard (4)
45PS.2    Boat club, The (3)
45PS.3    Brave Old Salt (48)
45PS.4    Do-somethings, The (29)
45PS.5    Fighting Joe (46)
45PS.6    In school and out (35)
45PS.7    Little by little (15)
45PS.8    Little merchant. The (18)
45PS.9    Now or never (5)
45PS.10   Poor and proud (9)
45PS.11   Proud and lazy (24)
45PS.12   Rich and humble (34)
45PS.13   Sailor boy, The (37)
45PS.14   Soldier boy, The (36)
45PS.15   Try again (6)
45PS.16   Watch and wait (40)
45PS.17   Work and win (45)
45PS.18   Yankee middy, The (44)
45PS.19   Young lieutenant, The (42)
```

46PS   THE OLIVER OPTIC BOOKS (New York Book Co.)

Series Description: Every boy and girl knows the Oliver
    Optic Books, and the New York Book Company's edition is
    the lowest priced cloth-bound edition. It is better in
    many ways than some of the higher priced editions. The
    covers are stamped in colors, in different and attractive
    designs. Frontispiece; decorated lining papers and title
    page; size five by seven and a quarter inches. [New York
    Book Co. ad].

46PS.1   Boat club, The (3)
46PS.2   All aboard (4)
46PS.3   Little by little (15)
46PS.4   Now or never (5)
46PS.5   Poor and proud (9)
46PS.6   Try again (6)
46PS.7   Fighting Joe (46)
46PS.8   Haste and waste (50)
46PS.9   Hope and have (49)
46PS.10   In school and out (35)
46PS.11   Rich and humble (34)
46PS.12   Work and win (45)

47PS   OLIVER OPTIC SERIES (Donohue)

Series Description: For a full generation the youth of Amer-
    ica has been reading and re-reading "Oliver Optic." No
    genuine boy ever tires of this famous author who knew just
    what boys wanted and was always able to supply his wants.
    Books are attractively bound in art shades of English
    vellum cloth, three designs stamped in three colors.
    Printed from large type on an extra quality of clean
    flexible paper. Each book in glazed paper wrapper.
    [Donohue ad].

Note: In later years, #15 Three millions , was removed from
    the list, with numbers 16-20 renumbered 15-19 respective-
    ly.

47PS.1   #1   All aboard (4)
47PS.2   #2   Brave Old Salt (48)
47PS.3   #3   Boat club, The (3)
47PS.4   #4   Fighting Joe (46)
47PS.5   #5   Haste and waste (50)
47PS.6   #6   Hope and have (49)
47PS.7   #7   In school and out (35)
47PS.8   #8   Little by little (15)
47PS.9   #9   Now or never (5)
47PS.10   #10 Outward bound (51)
47PS.11   #11 Poor and proud (9)
47PS.12   #12 Rich and humble (34)
47PS.13   #13 Sailor boy, The (37)
47PS.14   #14 Soldier boy, The (36)

```
47PS.15    #15    Three millions (53)
47PS.16    #16    Try again (6)
47PS.17    #17    Watch and wait (40)
47PS.18    #18    Work and win (45)
47PS.19    #19    Yankee middy, The (44)
47PS.20    #20    Young lieutenant, The (42)


48PS   OLIVER OPTIC SERIES   (Lee & Shepard;
          Lothrop, Lee & Shepard)

48PS.1     #1     Soldier boy, The (36)
48PS.2     #2     Young lieutenant, The (42)
48PS.3     #3     Fighting Joe (46)
48PS.4     #4     Sailor boy, The (37)
48PS.5     #5     Yankee middy, The (44)
48PS.6     #6     Brave Old Salt (48)
48PS.7     #7     Boat club, The (3)
48PS.8     #8     All aboard (4)
48PS.9     #9     Now or never (5)
48PS.10    #10    Try again (6)
48PS.11    #11    Poor and proud (9)
48PS.12    #12    Little by little (15)
48PS.13    #13    Through by daylight (66)
48PS.14    #14    Lightning Express (68)
48PS.15    #15    On time (69)
48PS.16    #16    Switch off (70)
48PS.17    #17    Brake up (71)
48PS.18    #18    Bear and forbear (74)
48PS.19    #19    Rich and humble (34)
48PS.20    #20    In school and out (35)
48PS.21    #21    Watch and wait (40)
48PS.22    #22    Work and win (45)
48PS.23    #23    Hope and have (49)
48PS.24    #24    Haste and waste (50)
48PS.25    #25    Starry flag, The (55)
48PS.26    #26    Breaking away (56)
48PS.27    #27    Seek and find (58)
48PS.28    #28    Freaks of fortune (61)
48PS.29    #29    Make or break (62)
48PS.30    #30    Down the river (64)
48PS.31    #31    Missing million, A (158)
48PS.32    #32    Millionaire at sixteen, A (159)
48PS.33    #33    Young knight-errant, A (161)
48PS.34    #34    Strange sights abroad (162)
48PS.35    #35    Outward bound (51)
48PS.36    #36    Shamrock and thistle (59)
48PS.37    #37    Red cross (60)
48PS.38    #38    Dikes and ditches (63)
48PS.39    #39    Palace and cottage (67)
48PS.40    #40    Down the Rhine (72)
48PS.41    #41    Up the Baltic (80)
48PS.42    #42    Northern lands (83)
48PS.43    #43    Cross and crescent (85)
48PS.44    #44    Sunny shores (93)
```

48PS.45 #45 Vine and olive (102)
48PS.46 #46 All adrift (120)
48PS.47 #47 Going west (98)
48PS.48 #48 Field and forest (75)
48PS.49 #49 Little Bobtail (84)
48PS.50 #50 Just his luck (105)

49PS OLIVER OPTIC'S BOAT CLUB SERIES
        (McLoughlin Brothers)

49PS.1 All aboard (4)
49PS.2 Boat club, The (3)
49PS.3 Now or never (5)

50PS OUR BOYS' PRIZE LIBRARY (Lee & Shepard;
        Charles T. Dillingham)

50PS.1 Just his luck (105)

51PS PRESIDENTIAL ELECTION CAMPAIGN BIOGRAPHIES
        (University Microfilms)

51PS.1 PE186 Our standard-bearer (65)

52PS ST. NICHOLAS SERIES (International Book Co.)

52PS.1 Nature's young nobleman (136)

53PS SCENES DE LA VIE AMERICAINE (Gedalge Jeune)

53PS.1 Boat club, The (3)

54PS SUPERIOR LIBRARY (Superior Printing Co.)

54PS.1 Outward bound (51)

55PS TABLEAUX DE LA VIE AMERICAINE (Gedale Jeune)

55PS.1 Try again (6)

56PS WANAMAKER'S YOUNG PEOPLE'S LIBRARY
        (John Wanamaker)

56PS.1 Poor and proud (9)

57PS WRIGHT AMERICAN FICTION (Research Publications)

57PS.1 Hatchie, the guardian slave (1)
57PS.2 In doors and out (2)
57PS.3 Way of the world, The (52)
57PS.4 Living too fast (101)

58PS YOUNG AMERICA LIBRARY FOR BOYS (Hurst)

58PS.1   Little merchant, The (18)
58PS.2   Watch and wait (40)
58PS.3   Young lieutenant, The (42)
58PS.4   In school and out (35)
58PS.5   Little by little (15)
58PS.6   Rich and humble (34)
58PS.7   Brave Old Salt (48)
58PS.8   Fighting Joe (45)
58PS.9   Yankee middy, The (44)
58PS.10 Work and win (45)

PUBLISHERS

Listed are the companies which published books and magazines written by William T. Adams, both originally and in reprint. The number in parenthesis refers to the CHRONOLOGICAL LIST entry number. All titles issued by each publisher are alphabetically arranged.

1P   JOSEPH H. ALLEN   Boston

1P.1   Student and schoolmate, The (7)

2P   AMERICAN NEWS CO.   New York

2P.1   All aboard (4)
2P.2   Boat club, The (3)
2P.3   Now or never (5)
2P.4   Try again (6)

3P   AMERICAN PUBLISHERS CORP.   New York

3P.1   Casket of diamonds, The (142)

4P   WALTER H. BAKER & CO.   Boston

4P.1   Voyage of life, The (57)

5P   BOOKS FOR LIBRARIES PRESS   Freeport, NY

5P.1   Hatchie, the guardian slave (1)

6P   BREWER & TILESTON   Boston

6P.1   Spelling book for advanced classes, A (32)

7P BROWN, BAZIN AND CO. Boston

7P.1   All aboard (4)
7P.2   Boat club, The (3)
7P.3   In doors and out (2)
7P.4   Now or never (5)

8P BROWN, TAGGARD AND CHASE Boston

8P.1   Boat club, The (3)
8P.2   Try again (6)
8P.3   Universal speaker, The (13)

9P A.L. BURT CO. New York

9P.1   All aboard (4)
9P.2   Boat club, The (3)
9P.3   Brave Old Salt 48)
9P.4   Fighting Joe (46)
9P.5   In school and out (35)
9P.6   Little by little (15)
9P.7   Now or never (5)
9P.8   Poor and proud (9)
9P.9   Rich and humble (34)
9P.10   Sailor boy, The (37)
9P.11   Soldier boy, The (36)
9P.12   Try again (6)
9P.13   Watch and wait (40)
9P.14   Work and win (45)
9P.15   Yankee middy, The (44)
9P.16   Young lieutenant, The (42)

10P   J.H. BUTLER & CO.   Philadelphia

10P.1   Spelling book for advanced classes, A (32)

11P   H.M. CALDWELL CO.   New York and Boston

11P.1   All aboard (4)
11P.2   Boat club, The (3)
11P.3   Just his luck (105)
11P.4   Little by little (15)
11P.5   Now or never (5)
11P.6   Poor and proud (9)
11P.7   Try again (6)

12P   CARLTON PRESS New York

12P.1   Boat club, The (3)

13P CASSELL, PETTER AND GALPIN
       London and New York

13P.1   Boat club, The (3)

14P W.B. CONKEY CO. Hammond,
       Indiana and Chicago

14P.1   All aboard (4)
14P.2   Boat club, The (3)
14P.3   Christmas gift, The (20)
14P.4   In school and out (35)
14P.5   Little by little (15)
14P.6   Little merchant, The (18)
14P.7   Now or never (5)
14P.8   Poor and proud (9)
14P.9   Rich and humble (34)
14P.10   Try again (6)

15P G.W. COTTRELL Boston

15P.1   Sports and pastimes for indoors and out (30)

16P CROSBY, NICHOLS, LEE Boston

16P.1   All aboard (4)
16P.2   Boat club, The (3)
16P.3   Little by little (15)
16P.4   Now or never (5)
16P.5   Poor and proud (9)
16P.6   Try again (6)

17P E.R. CURTIS Cincinnati, Ohio

17P.1   Little blossoms in the garden of home (154)

18P DeWOLFE & FISKE CO. Boston

18P.1   Charades and pantomimes (188)
18P.2   Popular amusements for school and home (189)

19P M.A. DONOHUE AND CO. Chicago and New York

19P.1   All aboard (4)
19P.2   Boat club, The (3)
19P.3   Brave Old Salt (48)
19P.4   Casket of diamonds, The (142)
19P.5   Fighting Joe (46)
19P.6   Haste and waste (50)
19P.7   Hope and have (49)

```
19P.8    In school and out (35)
19P.9    Little by little (15)
19P.10   Now or never (5)
19P.11   Outward bound (51)
19P.12   Poor and proud (9)
19P.13   Rich and humble (34)
19P.14   Sailor boy, The (37)
19P.15   Soldier boy, The (36)
19P.16   Three millions (53)
19P.17   Try again (6)
19P.18   Watch and wait (40)
19P.19   Work and win (45)
19P.20   Yankee middy, The (44)
19P.21   Young lieutenant, The (42)
```

20P DONOHUE & HENNEBERRY Chicago

```
20P.1    Boat club, The (3)
```

21P ESTES & LAURIAT Boston

```
21P.1    Oliver Optic's annual (117)
21P.2    Our little one's annual (169)
```

22P FEDERAL BOOK CO. New York

```
22P.1    All aboard (4)
22P.2    Boat club, The (3)
22P.3    Giant islanders, The (146)
22P.4    How he won (139)
22P.5    Little by little (15)
22P.6    Nature's young noblemen (136)
22P.7    Now or never (5)
22P.8    Poor and proud (9)
22P.9    Rival battalions, The (148)
22P.10   Try again (6)
22P.11   Young actor, The (152)
```

23P GEDALGE JEUNE Paris

```
23P.1    Boat club, The (3)
23P.2    Try again (6)
```

24P HENNEBERRY CO. Chicago

```
24P.1    All aboard (4)
24P.2    Boat club, The (3)
24P.3    Little by little (15)
24P.4    Now or never (5)
24P.5    Poor and proud (9)
24P.6    Try again (6)
```

25P HIGGINS AND BRADLEY Boston

25P.1   In doors and out (2)

26P HIGGINS, BRADLEY AND DAYTON Boston

26P.1   In doors and out (2)

27P HOMEWOOD PUBLISHING CO.   South Bend, IN

27P.1   All aboard (4)
27P.2   Boat club, The (3)
27P.3   Little by little (15)
27P.4   Now or never (5)
27P.5   Poor and proud (9)
27P.6   Try again (6)

28P HURST AND CO. New York

28P.1   All aboard (4)
28P.2   Birthday party, The (23)
            (with other titles)
28P.3   Boat club, The (3)
28P.4   Brave Old Salt (48)
28P.5   Careless Kate (25)
28P.6   Christmas gift, The (20)
            (with other titles)
28P.7   Do-somethings, The (29)
            (with other titles)
28P.8   Dolly and I (21)
            (with other titles)
28P.9   Fighting Joe (46)
28P.10   Gold thimble, The (28)
            (with other titles)
28P.11   Haste and waste (50)
28P.12   Hope and have (49)
28P.13   In school and out (35)
28P.14   Little by little (15)
28P.15   Little merchant, The (18)
            (with other titles)
28P.16   Now or never (5)
28P.17   Oliver Optic's new story book (180)
28P.18   Outward bound (51)
28P.19   Picnic party, The (27)
            (with other titles)
28P.20   Poor and proud (9)
28P.21   Proud and lazy (24)
            (with other titles)
28P.22   Rich and humble (34)
28P.23   Robinson Crusoe, Jr. (26)
28P.24   Sailor boy, The (37)
28P.25   Soldier boy, The (36)
28P.26   Try again (6)

28P.27   Uncle Ben (22)
28P.28   Watch and wait (40)
28P.29   Work and win (45)
28P.30   Yankee middy, The (44)
28P.31   Young lieutenant, The (42)
28P.32   Young voyagers, The (19)

29P   INTERNATIONAL BOOK CO.   New York

29P.1   All aboard (4)
29P.2   Boat club, The (3)
29P.3   Nature's young nobleman (136)
29P.4   Now or never (5)

30P   GALEN JAMES AND CO.   Boston

30P.1   Student and schoolmate, The (7)

31P   LEE & SHEPARD   Boston

31P.1   Across India (171)
31P.2   All aboard (4)
31P.3   All adrift (120)
31P.4   All taut (133)
31P.5   American boys afloat (163)
31P.6   Asiatic breezes (167)
31P.7   At the front (178)
31P.8   Bear and forbear (74)
31P.9   Birthday party (23)
31P.10   Bivouac and battle (81)
31P.11   Boat club, The (3)
31P.12   Brake up (71)
31P.13   Brave Old Salt (48)
31P.14   Breaking away (56)
31P.15   Brother against brother (168)
31P.16   Careless Kate (25)
31P.17   Christmas gift, The (20)
31P.18   Coming wave, The (91)
31P.19   Cringle and cross-tree (79)
31P.20   Cross and crescent (85)
31P.21   Desk and debit (77)
31P.22   Dikes and ditches (63)
31P.23   Do-somethings, The (29)
31P.24   Dolly and I (21)
31P.25   Dorcas Club, The (92)
31P.26   Down south (111)
31P.27   Down the Rhine (72)
31P.28   Down the river (64)
31P.29   Field and forest (75)
31P.30   Fighting for the right (160)
31P.31   Fighting Joe (46)
31P.32   Four young explorers (176)
31P.33   Freaks of fortune (61)

31P.34   Getting an indorser (95)
31P.35   Going south (109)
31P.36   Going west (98)
31P.37   Gold thimble, The (28)
31P.38   Great bonanza, The (99)
31P.39   Half round the world (172)
31P.40   Haste and waste (50)
31P.41   Hope and have (49)
31P.42   In doors and out (2)
31P.43   In school and out (35)
31P.44   In the saddle (170)
31P.45   Isles of the sea (106)
31P.46   Just his luck (105)
31P.47   Lake breezes (107)
31P.48   Lieutenant at eighteen, A (173)
31P.49   Lightning Express (68)
31P.50   Little Bobtail (84)
31P.51   Little by little (15)
31P.52   Little merchant, The (18)
31P.53   Living too fast (101)
31P.54   Make or break (62)
31P.55   Millionaire at sixteen, A (159)
31P.56   Missing million, A (158)
31P.57   Money-maker (89)
31P.58   Northern lands (83)
31P.59   Now or never (5)
31P.60   Ocean-born (96)
31P.61   Oliver Optic's almanac (78)
31P.62   Oliver Optic's Magazine (54)
31P.63   On the blocade (155)
31P.64   On the staff (175)
31P.65   On time (69)
31P.66   Our boys and girls album (54g)
31P.67   Our boys and girls cabinet (54i)
31P.68   Our boys and girls companion (54c)
31P.69   Our boys and girls favorite (54b)
31P.70   Our boys and girls keepsake (54f)
31P.71   Our boys and girls mirror (54j)
31P.72   Our boys and girls museum (54h)
31P.73   Our boys and girls offering (54k)
31P.74   Our boys and girls repository (54e)
31P.75   Our boys and girls souvenir (54l)
31P.76   Our boys and girls storyteller (54a)
31P.77   Our boys and girls treasure (54d)
31P.78   Our standard-bearer (65)
31P.79   Out west (103)
31P.80   Outward bound (51)
31P.81   Pacific shores (177)
31P.82   Palace and cottage (67)
31P.83   Picnic party, The (27)
31P.84   Plane and plank (76)
31P.85   Poor and proud (9)
31P.86   Proud and lazy (24)
31P.87   Ready about (138)
31P.88   Red cross (60)
31P.89   Rich and humble (34)

31P.90   Robinson Crusoe, Jr. (26)
31P.91   Sailor boy, The (37)
31P.92   Sea and shore (82)
31P.93   Seek and find (58)
31P.94   Shamrock and thistle (59)
31P.95   Snug Harbor (125)
31P.96   Soldier boy, The (36)
31P.97   Square and compasses (128)
31P.98   Stand by the Union (157)
31P.99   Starry flag, The (55)
31P.100   Stem to stern (131)
31P.101   Strange sights abroad (162)
31P.102   Sunny shores (93)
31P.103   Switch off (70)
31P.104   Taken by the enemy (145)
31P.105   Three millions (53)
31P.106   Through by daylight (66)
31P.107   Try again (6)
31P.108   Uncle Ben (22)
31P.109   Undivided union (179)
31P.110   Up and down the Nile (166)
31P.111   Up the Baltic (80)
31P.112   Up the river (114)
31P.113   Victorious union, A (164)
31P.114   Vine and olive (102)
31P.115   Watch and wait (40)
31P.116   Way of the world, The (52)
31P.117   Within the enemy's lines (149)
31P.118   Work and win (45)
31P.119   Yacht club, The (87)
31P.120   Yankee middy, The (44)
31P.121   Young folks' Robinson Crusoe (113)
31P.122   Young knight-errant, A (161)
31P.123   Young lieutenant, The (42)
31P.124   Young navigators, The (165)
31P.125   Young voyagers, The (19)

32P LEE & SHEPARD, Boston; CHARLES T. DILLINGHAM,
     New York

32P.1   All aboard (4)
32P.2   All adrift (120)
32P.3   All taut (133)
32P.4   Birthday party, The (23)
32P.5   Bivouac and battle (81)
32P.6   Boat club, The (3)
32P.7   Brave Old Salt (48)
32P.8   Breaking away (56)
32P.9   Careless Kate (25)
32P.10   Christmas gift, The (20)
32P.11   Cringle and cross-tree (79)
32P.12   Desk and debit (77)
32P.13   Do-somethings, The (29)
32P.14   Dolly and I (21)
32P.15   Dorcas Club, The (92)

32P.16   Down south (111)
32P.17   Field and forest (75)
32P.18   Fighting Joe (46)
32P.19   Freaks of fortune (61)
32P.20   Going south (109)
32P.21   Going west (98)
32P.22   Gold thimble, The (28)
32P.23   Great bonanza, The (99)
32P.24   Just his luck (105)
32P.25   Isles of the sea (106)
32P.26   Lake breezes (107)
32P.27   Lightning Express (68)
32P.28   Little by little (15)
32P.29   Little merchant, The (18)
32P.30   Living too fast (101)
32P.31   Now or never (5)
32P.32   Ocean-born (96)
32P.33   On the staff (155)
32P.34   On time (69)
32P.35   Our standard-bearer (65)
32P.36   Out west (103)
32P.37   Picnic party, The (27)
32P.38   Plane and plank (76)
32P.39   Poor and proud (9)
32P.40   Proud and lazy (24)
32P.41   Ready about (138)
32P.42   Red cross (60)
32P.43   Rich and humble (34)
32P.44   Robinson Crusoe, Jr. (26)
32P.45   Sailor boy, The (37)
32P.46   Sea and shore (82)
32P.47   Seek and find (53)
32P.48   Shamrock and thistle (59)
32P.49   Snug Harbor (125)
32P.50   Soldier boy, The (36)
32P.51   Square and compasses (128)
32P.52   Stand by the Union (157)
32P.53   Starry flag, The (55)
32P.54   Stem to stern (131)
32P.55   Switch off (70)
32P.56   Taken by the enemy (145)
32P.57   Through by daylight (66)
32P.58   Try again (6)
32P.59   Uncle Ben (22)
32P.60   Up the river (114)
32P.61   Vine and olive (102)
32P.62   Within the enemy's lines (149)
32P.63   Young lieutenant, The (42)
32P.64   Young voyagers, The (19)

33P LEE & SHEPARD, Boston; LEE, SHEPARD
        & DILLINGHAM, New York

33P.1   All aboard (4)
33P.2   Bear and forbear (74)

33P.3   Bivouac and battle (81)
33P.4   Boat club, The (3)
33P.5   Brake up (71)
33P.6   Brave Old Salt (48)
33P.7   Breaking away (56)
33P.8   Coming wave, The (91)
33P.9   Cringle and cross-tree (79)
33P.10 Cross and crescent (85)
33P.11 Desk and debit (77)
33P.12 Dikes and ditches (63)
33P.13 Dorcas Club, The (92)
33P.14 Down the Rhine (72)
33P.15 Down the river (64)
33P.16 Field and forest (75)
33P.17 Great bonanza, The (99)
33P.18 Haste and waste (50)
33P.19 Hope and have (49)
33P.20 In school and out (35)
33P.21 Lightning Express (68)
33P.22 Little Bobtail (84)
33P.23 Little by little (15)
33P.24 Make or break (62)
33P.25 Money-maker, The (89)
33P.26 Northern lands (83)
33P.27 Now or never (5)
33P.28 Ocean-born (96)
33P.29 Outward bound (51)
33P.30 Palace and cottage (67)
33P.31 Plane and plank (76)
33P.32 Poor and proud (9)
33P.33 Red cross (60)
33P.34 Sea and shore (82)
33P.35 Shamrock and thistle (59)
33P.36 Sunny shores (93)
33P.37 Through by daylight (66)
33P.38 Try again (6)
33P.39 Up the Baltic (80)
33P.40 Way of the world, The (52)
33P.41 Work and win (45)
33P.42 Yacht club, The (87)
33P.43 Yankee middy, The (44)
33P.44 Young lieutenant, The (42)

34P   J.B. LIPPINCOTT CO.   Philadelphia

34P.1   Rich and humble (34)

35P   LOG CABIN PRESS

35P.1   Outward bound (5)

36P LOTHROP, LEE & SHEPARD   Boston

36P.1   Across India (171)
36P.2   All aboard (4)
36P.3   All adrift (120)
36P.4   All taut (133)
36P.5   Always in luck (135)
36P.6   American boys afloat (163)
36P.7   Among the missing (153)
36P.8   Asiatic breezes (167)
36P.9   At the front (178)
36P.10   Bear and forbear (74)
36P.11   Birthday party, The (23)
36P.12   Bivouac and battle (81)
36P.13   Boat club, The (3)
36P.14   Brake up (71)
36P.15   Brave Old Salt (48)
36P.16   Breaking away (56)
36P.17   Brother against brother (168)
36P.18   Building himself up (115)
36P.19   Careless Kate (25)
36P.20   Christmas gift, The (20)
36P.21   Coming wave, The (91)
36P.22   Cringle and cross-tree (79)
36P.23   Cross and crescent (85)
36P.24   Cruise of the Dandy, The (141)
36P.25   Desk and debit (77)
36P.26   Dikes and ditches (63)
36P.27   Do-somethings, The (29)
36P.28   Dolly and I (21)
36P.29   Dorcas Club, The (92)
36P.30   Down south (111)
36P.31   Down the Rhine (72)
36P.32   Down the river (64)
36P.33   Every inch a boy (127)
36P.34   Field and forest (75)
36P.35   Fighting for the right (160)
36P.36   Fighting Joe (46)
36P.37   Four young explorers (176)
36P.38   Freaks of fortune (61)
36P.39   Going south (109)
36P.40   Going west (98)
36P.41   Gold thimble, The (28)
36P.42   Half round the world (172)
36P.43   Haste and waste (50)
36P.44   His own helper (132)
36P.45   Honest Kit Dunstable (186)
36P.46   Hope and have (49)
36P.47   In school and out (35)
36P.48   In the saddle (170)
36P.49   In doors and out (2)
36P.50   Isles of the sea (106)
36P.51   Just his luck (105)
36P.52   Lake breezes (107)
36P.53   Lieutenant at eighteen, A (173)
36P.54   Lightning Express (68)

36P.111   Up the river (114)
36P.112   Victorious union, A (164)
36P.113   Vine and olive (102)
36P.114   Watch and wait (40)
36P.115   Within the enemy's lines (149)
36P.116   Work and win (45)
36P.117   Yacht club, The (87)
36P.118   Yankee middy, The (44)
36P.119   Young hermit of Lake Minnetonka, The (144)
36P.120   Young knight-errant, A (161)
36P.121   Young lieutenant, The (42)
36P.122   Young navigators, The (165)
36P.123   Young pilot, The (187)
36P.124   Young voyagers, The (19)

37P   FRANK F. LOVELL & CO.   New York

37P.1   Nature's young noblemen (136)

38P   F.M. LUPTON   New York

38P.1   All aboard (4)
38P.2   Boat club, The (3)

39P   DAVID McKAY   Philadelphia

39P.1   All aboard (4)
39P.2   Boat club, The (3)
39P.3   Giant islanders, The (146)
39P.4   How he won (139)
39P.5   Little by little (15)
39P.6   Nature's young nobleman (136)
39P.7   Now or never (5)
39P.8   Rival battalions, The (148)
39P.9   Try again (6)
39P.10   Young actor, The (152)

40P   MacLELLAN COMPANY   Akron, Ohio

40P.1   Outward bound (51)

41P   McLOUGHLIN BROTHERS   New York

41P.1   All aboard (4)
41P.2   Boat club, The (3)
41P.3   Little by little (15)
41P.4   Now or never (5)
41P.5   Try again (6)

42P   J.S. MARR   Glasgow, Scotland

42P.1   Adventures of a midshipman, The (129)

43P   MERSHON COMPANY   Rahway, NJ and New York

43P.1   All aboard (4)
43P.2   Boat club, The (3)
43P.3   Little by little (15)
43P.4   Now or never (5)
43P.5   Poor and proud (9)
43P.6   Try again (6)

44P   GEORGE MUNRO'S SONS   New York

44P.1   Boat club, The (3)

45P   FRANK A. MUNSEY CO.   New York

45P.1   Nature's young nobleman (136)

46P   B.B. MUSSEY AND CO. AND R.B. FITTS   Boston

46P.1   Hatchie, the guardian slave (1)

47P   NEW YORK BOOK CO.   New York

47P.1   All aboard (4)
47P.2   Boat club, The (3)
47P.3   Fighting Joe (46)
47P.4   Haste and waste (50)
47P.5   Hope and have (49)
47P.6   In school and out (35)
47P.7   Little by little (15)
47P.8   Now or never (5)
47P.9   Poor and proud (9)
47P.10 Rich and humble (34)
47P.11 Try again (6)
47P.12 Work and win (45)

48P   NEW YORK PUBLISHING CO.   New York

48P.1   Boat club, The (3)
48P.2   Now or never (5)
48P.3   Poor and proud (9)

49P   J.S. OGILVIE PUBLISHING CO.   New York

49P.1   All aboard (4)

49P.2   Boat club, The (3)
49P.3   Little by little (15)
49P.4   Now or never (5)
49P.5   Poor and proud (9)

50P   R.S. PEALE   Chicago

50P.1   Holiday joys for bright girls and boys (150)
50P.2   Story and song. For all winter long (151)

51P   S.C. PERKINS   Boston

51P.1   Try again (6)

52P   PHILLIPS, SAMPSON & CO.   Boston

52P.1   All aboard (4)
52P.2   Boat club, The (3)
52P.3   Now or never (5)
52P.4   Poor and proud (9)
52P.5   Try again (6)

53P   RESEARCH PUBLICATIONS   Woodbridge, CT

53P.1   Hatchie, the guardian slave (1)
53P.2   In doors and out (2)
53P.3   Living too fast (101)
53P.4   Way of the world, The (52)

54P   J.W. RICHARDSON   Boston

54P.1   Standard historical stories (73)

55P   RICKEY, MALLORY; CROSBY, NICHOLS, LEE;
        PHINNEY, BLAKEMAN & MASON   Cincinnati, Ohio

55P.1   All aboard (4)
55P.2   Boat club, The (3)
55P.3   Little by little (15)
55P.4   Now or never (5)
55P.5   Poor and proud (9)
55P.6   Try again (6)

56P   JAMES ROBINSON & CO.   Boston

56P.1   Student and schoolmate, The (7)

57P ROBINSON, GREENE & CO. Boston

57P.1   Student and schoolmate, The (7)

58P RUSSELL PUBLISHING CO. Boston

58P.1   Oliver Optic's annual (117)
58P.2   Our little ones and the nursery (118)

59P SAALFIELD PUBLISHING CO. Chicago, Akron
        and New York

59P.1   Little by little (15)
59P.2   Young lieutenant, The (42)

60P STREET & SMITH New York

60P.1   All aboard (4)
60P.2   Always in luck (135)
60P.3   Among the missing (153)
60P.4   Bear and forbear (74)
60P.5   Boat club, The (3)
60P.6   Brake up (71)
60P.7   Brave Old Salt (48)
60P.8   Breaking away (56)
60P.9   Building himself up (115)
60P.10   Cruise of the Dandy, The (141)
60P.11   Down the river (64)
60P.12   Every inch a boy (127)
60P.13   Freaks of fortune (61)
60P.14   Giant islanders, The (146)
60P.15   Haste and waste (50)
60P.16   His own helper (132)
60P.17   Honest Kit Dunstable (186)
60P.18   Hope and have (49)
60P.19   How he won (139)
60P.20   In school and out (35)
60P.21   Lightning Express (68)
60P.22   Little by little (15)
60P.23   Louis Chiswick's mission (182)
60P.24   Lyon Hart's heroism (183)
60P.25   Make or break (62)
60P.26   Making a man of himself (124)
60P.27   Nature's young nobleman (136)
60P.28   Nature's young noblemen (136)
60P.29   Now or never (5)
60P.30   On time (69)
60P.31   Poor and proud (9)
60P.32   Prisoners of the cave, The (147)
60P.33   Professor's son, The (126)
60P.34   Rich and humble (34)
60P.35   Rival battalions, The (148)
60P.36   Royal Tarr's pluck (184)

```
60P.37   Sailor boy, The (37)
60P.38   Seek and find (58)
60P.39   Starry flag, The (55)
60P.40   Striving for his own (185)
60P.41   Switch off (70)
60P.42   Three young silver kings (137)
60P.43   Through by daylight (66)
60P.44   Try again (6)
60P.45   Watch and wait (40)
60P.46   Work and win (45)
60P.47   Yankee middy, The (44)
60P.48   Young actor, The (152)
60P.49   Young hermit, The (144)
60P.50   Young pilot, The (187)
```

61P SUPERIOR PRINTING CO.   Akron and New York

61P.1   Outward bound (51)

62P TAGGARD AND THOMPSON   Boston

62P.1   Universal speaker, The (13)

63P TAIT, SONS & CO.   New York

63P.1   Young actor, The (152)

64P THAYER AND ELDRIDGE   Boston

64P.1   Marrying a beggar (11)

65P THAYER, MERRIAM & CO.   Philadelphia

65P.1   Little blossoms in the garden of home (154)

66P N.D. THOMPSON PUBLISHING CO.   St. Louis

66P.1   Holiday joys for bright girls and boys (150)
66P.2   Story and song. For all winter long (151)

67P THOMPSON & THOMAS AND C.C. THOMPSON CO.   Chicago

67P.1   Casket of diamonds, The (142)

68P UNITED STATES BOOK CO.   New York

68P.1   Casket of diamonds, The (142)
68P.2   How he won (139)

68P.3   Rival battalions, The (148)
68P.4   Young actor, The (152)

69P   UNIVERSITY MICROFILMS INTERNATIONAL
        Ann Arbor, Michigan

69P.1   Our standard-bearer (65)

70P   JOHN WANAMAKER   Philadelphia

70P.1   Poor and proud (9)

71P   WARD & LOCK   London

71P.1   Adventures of a midshipman, The (129)
71P.2   Brave Old Salt (48)

72P   WILLIAM WARE   Boston

72P.1   Spelling book for advanced classes, A (32)

73P   WENTWORTH, HEWES & CO.   Boston

73P.1   Marrying a beggar (11)

SERIALIZATIONS

Listed are those titles which appeared serially in magazines
and newspapers. Titles are listed in chronological order
under the magazine in which they appeared. The CHRONOLOGICAL
LIST entry number is in parenthesis following the title.
S = Serialization

1S AMERICAN BOY

1S.1   "That Dillingham boy" (181)
            November 1907 - February 1909

2S THE ARGOSY (see also THE GOLDEN ARGOSY)

2S.1   "The prisoners of the cave" (147)
            1 December 1888 - 23 February 1889
2S.2   "The rival battalions" by Brooks McCormick (148)
            9 March - 22 June 1889
2S.3   "The young actor" by Gayle Winterton (152)
            2 November 1889 - 15 February 1890
2S.4   "Among the missing" (153)
            18 January - 17 May 1890

3S THE BANNER WEEKLY

3S.1   "The pink of the Pacific: or, The adventures of a
        stowaway" (108)
            v.2 #58-71 (22 December 1883 - 22 March 1884)
            v.8 #380-393 (22 February - 24 May 1890)
        "The pink of the Pacific: or, Running down the
        kidnappers" (108)
            v.14 #706-720 (23 May - 29 August 1896)

4S   BOSTON DAILY GLOBE

4S.1   "Beau Gray: or, Getting his living" (116)
        2 January - 4 February 1882

5S   BOSTON WEEKLY GLOBE

5S.1   "Dunn Brown and his double" (119)
        25 April - 23 May 1882

     FIRESIDE COMPANION
     see NEW YORK FIRESIDE COMPANION

6S   THE GOLDEN ARGOSY (see also THE ARGOSY)

6S.1   "Making a man of himself" (124)
        20 October 1883 - 26 January 1884
6S.2   "Every inch a boy" (127)
        30 August - 8 November 1884
6S.3   "Always in luck" (135)
        15 January - 23 April 1887
6S.4   "Nature's young nobleman" by Brooks McCormick (136)
        26 February - 4 June 1887
6S.5   "How he won" by Brooks McCormick (139)
        15 October - 24 December 1887
6S.6   "The young pilot of Lake Montoban" (140)
        22 October - 19 November 1887
6S.7   "The cruise of 'The Dandy'" (141)
        3 December 1887 - 10 March 1888
6S.8   "The casket of diamonds" by Gayle Winterton (142)
        31 March - 14 July 1888
6S.9   "The young hermit of Lake Minnetonka" (144)
        19 May - 8 September 1888
6S.10   "The giant islanders" by Brooks McCormick (146)
        6 October - 15 December 1888

7S   GOLDEN DAYS FOR BOYS AND GIRLS

7S.1   "Minding his own business" (110)
        v.1 #20-32 (17 July - 9 October 1880)
        v.9 #23-35 (5 May - 28 July 1888)
7S.2   "Lost-on island" (112)
        v.1 #38 - v.2 #12 (20 November 1880 - 26 February
        1881)
        v.18 #45 - v.19 #7 (25 September 1897 - 1 January
        1898)
7S.3   "Building himself up: or, The cruise of the 'Fish
        Hawk'" (115)

          v.2 #42-52 (24 September - 17 December 1881)
          v.17 #21-31 (April 11 - June 20, 1896)
7S.4   "Lyon Hart: or, Adrift in the world" (121)
          v.4 #1-12 (9 December 1882 - 24 February 1883)
          v.17 #45 - v.18 #4 (26 September - 12 December
          1896)
7S.5   "Louis Chiswick: or, Going with the current" (122)
          v.4 #20-31 (21 April - 7 July 1883)
          v.18 #4-15 (12 December 1896 - 27 February 1897)
7S.6   "Royal Tarr: or, Learning to live" (123)
          v.4 #33-44 (21 July - 6 October 1883)
          v.18 #18-29 (20 March - 5 June 1897)
7S.7   "The professor's son: or, The triumphs of a young
          athlete" (126)
          v.5 #29-40 (21 June - 6 September 1884)
          v.20 #31-42 (17 June - 2 September 1899)
7S.8   "Fighting for his own" (130)
          v.6 #25-36 (23 May - 8 August 1885)
          v.21 #5-16 (16 December 1899 - 3 March 1900)
7S.9   "His own helper: or, Doing for himself" (132)
          v.7 #3-14 (19 December 1885 - 6 March 1886)
          v.22 #18-29 (16 March - 1 June 1901)
7S.10   "Kit Dunstable: or, A watch for nothing" (134)
          v.8 #7-18 (15 January - 2 April 1887)
          v.21 #35-46 (14 July - 29 September 1900)
7S.11   "Three young silver kings" (137)
          v.8 #26-39 (28 May - 27 August 1887)
          v.21 #46 - v.22 #6 (29 September - 22 December
          1900)

8S   GOOD NEWS

8S.1   "Nothing but a boy" (104)
          20 December 1890 - 28 March 1891

9S   MUNRO'S GIRLS AND BOYS OF AMERICA

9S.1   "The amateur detective" (100)
          25 March - 15 July 1876

10S   NEW YORK FIRESIDE COMPANION

10S.1   "A brave boy's fortune" (88)
          17 March - 30 June 1873
10S.2   "Mending his ways" (97)
          24 May - 20 September 1875

11S   NEW YORK SATURDAY JOURNAL

11S.1   "The pink of the Pacific: or, The adventures
         of a stowaway" (108)
              v.10 #481-484 (31 May - 21 June 1879)

12S   NEW YORK WEEKLY

12S.1   "Nothing but a boy" (104)
              16 July 1877 - ???

13S   OLIVER OPTIC'S MAGAZINE

13S.1   "The starry flag: or, The young fisherman of Cape
         Ann" (55)
              v.1 #1-26 (5 January - 29 June 1867)
13S.2   "Breaking away: or, The fortunes of a student" (56)
              v.2 #27-39 (6 July - 28 September 1867)
13S.3   "The voyage of life: an allegory" co-written with
         George M. Baker (57)
              v.2 #32-33 (10-17 August 1867)
13S.4   "Seek and find: or, The adventures of a smart boy"
         (58)
              v.2 #40-52 (5 October - 28 December 1867)
13S.5   "Freaks of fortune: or, Half round the world" (61)
              v.3 #53-65 (4 January - 28 March 1868)
13S.6   "Make or break: or, The rich man's daughter" (62)
              v.3 #66-78 (4 April - 27 June 1868)
13S.7   "Down the river: or, Buck Bradford and his tyrants"
         (64)
              v.4 #79-91 (4 July - 26 September 1868)
13S.8   "Through by daylight: or, The young engineer of the
         Lake Shore Railroad" (66)
              v.4 #92-104 (3 October - 26 December 1868)
13S.9   "Lightning Express: or, The rival academies" (68)
              v.5 #105-117 (2 January - 27 March 1869)
13S.10   "On time: or, The young captain of the Ucayga
         steamer" (69)
              v.5 #118-130 (3 April - 26 June 1869)
13S.11   "Switch off: or, The war of the students" (70)
              v.6 #131-143 (3 July - 25 September 1869)
13S.12   "Brake up: or, The young peacemakers" (71)
              v.6 #144-156 (2 October - 25 December 1869)
13S.13   "Bear and forbear: or, The young skipper of Lake
         Ucayga" (74)
              v.7 #157-169 (1 January - 26 March 1870)
13S.14   "Field and forest: or, The fortunes of a farmer" (75)
              v.7 #170-182 (2 April - 25 June 1870)
13S.15   "Plane and plank: or, The mishaps of a mechanic" (76)
              v.8 #183-195 (2 July - 24 September 1870)
13S.16   "Desk and debit: or, The catastrophes of a clerk"
         (77)

```
           v.8 #196-209 (1 October - 31 December 1870)
13S.17  "Cringle and cross-tree: or, The sea swashes of a
        sailor" (79)
           v.9 #210-215 (January - June 1871)
13S.18  "Bivouac and battle: or, The struggles of a soldier"
        (81)
           v.10 #216-221 (July - December 1871)
13S.19  "Sea and shore: or, The tramps of a traveller" (82)
           v.11 #222-227 (January - June 1872)
13S.20  "Little Bobtail: or, The wreck of the Penobscot" (84)
           v.12 #228-233 (July - December 1872)
13S.21  "The yacht club: or, The young boat-builder" (87)
           v.13 #234-239 (January - June 1873)
13S.22  "Money-maker: or, The victory of the Basilisk" (89)
           v.14 #240-245 (July - December 1873)
13S.23  "The coming wave: or, The hidden treasure of High
        Rock" (91)
           v.15 #246-251 (January - June 1874)
13S.24  "The Dorcas Club: or, Our girls afloat" (92)
           v.16 #252-257 (July - December 1874)
13S.25  "Ocean-born: or, The cruise of the clubs" (96)
           v.17 #258-263 (January - June 1875)
13S.26  "Going west: or, The perils of a poor boy" (98)
           v.18 #264-269 (July - December 1875)


14S  OUR YOUNG FOLKS

14S.1   "The cruise of the Leopold: or, The fortunes of a
        good-for-nothing" (43)
           v.1 #10-12 (October - December 1865)



        THE SATURDAY JOURNAL
        see NEW YORK SATURDAY JOURNAL



15S  THE STUDENT AND SCHOOLMATE

15S.1   "Things worth knowing" (8)
           May - October 1858
15S.2   "The magic lantern: or, Winter evening lessons" (10)
           December 1858 - June 1859
15S.3   "Frank Howard's journey in the United States" (12)
           January - April, June - July 1859
15S.4   "The young philosopher" (14)
           January - December 1860
15S.5   "The young travelers" (16)
           January - August 1861
15S.6   "The widow and her son: a New Year's story" (17)
           January 1862 - ???
15S.7   "Live and learn: or, The adventures of Paul
        Clifford" (31)
```

January - June 1863

15S.8   "Onward and upward: or, Paul Clifford in search of a
         situation" (33)
         July - December 1863

15S.9   "Trials and triumphs: or, Paul Clifford in trouble"
         (38)
         January - June 1864

15S.10   "Work and play: or, Paul Clifford's vacation" (39)
         July - December 1864

15S.11   "Out in the world: or, Paul Clifford on a cruise"
         (41)
         January - December 1865

15S.12   "The club boat: or, The fairy archers of Islington"
         (47)
         January - December 1866

16S   YOUNG NEW YORKER

16S.1   "The Pink of the Pacific: or, The adventures of a
         stowaway" (108)
         v.1 #25 (10 May 1879) - end of volume. It was
         announced that the story would be continued in
         The [New York] Saturday Journal (11S), v.10 #483,
         but it was not.

APPENDIX A
SPECIAL COLLECTIONS DIRECTORY

The collections listed below have substantial holdings of works authored by William Taylor Adams. Arrangement is by NUC symbol, as used in the "Locations" section in the CHRONOLOGICAL LIST.

The number of volumes indicated for each collection is approximate, due to possible recent acquisitions. The total number of volumes include multiple editions of one title (i.e. four varying editions of The boat club count as four volumes rather than one).

CSmH
Rare Books Department
The Huntington Library
1151 Oxford Rd.
San Marino, CA 91108

75 volumes; 2 magazine titles

CtY
The Beinecke Rare Book and
  Manuscript Library
Yale University
Box 1603A Yale Station
New Haven, CT 06520

81 volumes; 2 magazine titles

DLC
Rare Books Division
Library of Congress
Washington, DC 20540

241 volumes; 3 magazine titles

FTS
Special Collections
The Library
University of South Florida
Tampa, FL 33620

112 volumes; 1 magazine title

FU
Baldwin Library
University of Florida
Gainesville, FL 32611

134 volumes; 3 magazine titles

GEU
Special Collections
Robert W. Woodruff Library
Emory University
Atlanta, GA 30322

51 volumes

IDekN
Rare Book Collection
The University Libraries
Northern Illinois University
DeKalb, IL 60115

92 volumes

KU
Dept. of Special Collections
Spencer Research Library
University of Kansas
Lawrence, KS 66045-2800

70 volumes; 2 magazine titles

MB
Research Library Collection
Boston Public Library
Boston, MA 02117

191 volumes; 3 magazine titles

[no NUC symbol]
Medway Public Library
26 High Street
Medway, MA 02053

69 volumes; 2 magazine titles
(this information was received
too late to be included in the
"Locations" listings).

MWA
American Antiquarian Society
185 Salisbury St.
Worcester, MA 01609-1634

136 volumes; 3 magazine titles

MWalB
Special Collections
Brandeis University Library
Brandeis University
Waltham, MA 02154

78 volumes

MiEM
Special Collections Division
Libraries
Michigan State University
East Lansing, MI 48824

62 volumes; 1 magazine title

MnU
Children's Literature
  Research Collection
109 Walter Library
University of Minnesota
Minneapolis, MN 55455

18 volumes (Kerlan Collection)
190 volumes; 1 magazine title
          (Series Book Collection)

MoS
Children's Literature Room
St. Louis Public Library
1301 Olive St.
St. Louis, MO 63103

41 volumes; 1 magazine title

MsHAu
de Grummond Collection
McCain Library and Archives
University of Southern
  Mississippi
S. S. Box 5148
Hattiesburg, MS 39406-5148

155 volumes; 2 magazine titles

NHD
Special Collections
Dartmouth College Library
Dartmouth College
Hanover, NH 03755

176 volumes

NN
General Research Division
New York Public Library
20 West 53rd St.
New York , NY 10019

159 volumes; 3 magazine titles

Nh
Historical Children's
  Collection
New Hampshire State Library
20 Park Street
Concord, NH 03301

122 volumes

OAU
Archives and Special
  Collections
Vernon R. Alden Library
Ohio University
Athens, OH 45701

77 volumes

OBgU
Popular Culture Collection
University Library
Bowling Green State University
Bowling Green, OH 43402

69 volumes

OC
The Public Library of
  Cincinnati and Hamilton Co.
800 Vine St.
Library Square
Cincinnati, OH 45202-2071

92 volumes; 2 magazine titles

PP
Central Children's Department
The Free Library of
  Philadelphia
Logan Square
Philadelphia, PA 19103

91 volumes; 1 magazine title

PPiU
The Elizabeth Nesbitt Room
School of Library and
  Information Science
University of Pittsburgh
Pittsburgh, PA 15260

33 volumes; 1 magazine title

TxU
Harry Ransom Humanities
  Research Center
University of Texas at Austin
Office of the Librarian
P.O. Drawer 7219
Austin, TX 78713-7219

70 volumes

ViU
Rare Book Department
Alderman Library
University of Virginia
Charlottesville, VA 22901

75 volumes

WM
Historical Children's Book
  Collection
Milwaukee Public Library
814 W. Wisconsin Ave.
Milwaukee, WI 53233

90 volumes; 2 magazine titles

WU
Cooperative Children's Book
  Center
Rooms 4289 and 4290
Helen C. White Hall
600 North Park St.
Madison, WI 53706

45 volumes

APPENDIX B
CHRONOLOGY OF WILLIAM TAYLOR ADAMS AND HIS PUBLISHERS

1822   William Taylor Adams born in Medway, MA on July 30.

1844   William Lee hired by Phillips, Sampson & Co. Became a partner in 1850.

1852   Adams received copyright on <u>Hatchie, the guardian slave</u> under pseudonym of Warren T. Ashton.

1854   Adams received copyright on <u>The boat club</u> , his first book for children.

1855   Charles A.B. Shepard left the John Jewett firm and created Shepard, Clark & Co., 110 Washington Street, Boston. Became Shepard, Clark & Brown in 1857.

1859   Dissolution of Shepard, Clark & Brown.

        Phillips and Sampson both died. Stock of books and stereotype plates auctioned on November 15, 1859. William Lee purchased some of the plates including Oliver Optic's juvenile books.

1860   William Lee joined Crosby, Nichols & Co. Name changed to Crosby, Nichols, Lee & Co. on Feb. 11, 1860. Firm published Oliver Optic books from plates Lee purchased at auction.

1861   Dissolution of Crosby, Nichols, Lee & Co. Name returns to Crosby & Nichols when Lee leaves firm.

1862   William Lee and Charles Shepard found Lee & Shepard publishers, 155 Washington Street, Boston on February 1, 1862.

        Lee & Shepard purchased stereotype plates from Samuel C. Perkins, one-time partner in Phillips, Sampson & Co.

        Lee & Shepard's first ad appeared in <u>American Literary Gazette</u> December 1, 1862.

Lee & Shepard moved their offices to 149 Washington Street in December.

1865   Adams resigned as principal of the Bowditch School in July.

Adams embarked on first European trip.

1867   Publication of <u>Oliver Optic's Magazine</u>, vol.1, no.1 January 5, 1867.

1870   Establishment of New York branch in conjunction with Charles T. Dillingham. Became Lee, Shepard & Dillingham with offices at 49 Green St, Boston.

1872   Great Boston Fire in November destroyed stock at Milk Street warehouse. Washington Street firm damaged.

1874   Lee & Shepard moved offices to 41-45 Franklin St.

1875   Failure of Lee & Shepard on August 28, 1875. Charles T. Dillingham bought out interest in the New York Lee, Shepard & Dillingham and resumed business as Charles T. Dillingham.

Louisa May Alcott attacked the sensational character of Optic books in "Eight Cousins," which appeared in <u>St. Nicholas</u> magazine January through October.

Public announcement of the failure of Lee & Shepard on August 28, 1875.

Lee & Shepard resumed business as agents of the Court of Bankruptcy in early November.

1881   Lee & Shepard moved offices to 27 Franklin Street.

1882   Lee & Shepard disposed of their retail and jobber business; transferred to an employee, Emery Cleaves.

1885   Lee & Shepard moved offices to 10 Milk Street.

1886   Adams moved to Minneapolis to start a business with his son-in-law.

1887   Twenty-fifth anniversary of Lee & Shepard.

1888   Adams returned to live in Massachusetts.

1889   Charles Shepard died January 25, 1889.

1896   Charles T. Dillingham retired.

1897   William Taylor Adams died March 27, 1897.

1898   William Lee retired.

1898   Estate of Edwin Fleming purchased all title and
        interest in Lee & Shepard.

1899   Lee & Shepard offices moved to 202 Devonshire St.,
        Boston.

1904   Lee & Shepard firm purchased assets of Lothrop Co.
        to form Lothrop, Lee & Shepard, August 1904.

1906   William Lee died November 30.

APPENDIX C
NONSERIES BOOKS

The following titles were never issued as a part of an author series created by William Taylor Adams.

Adventures of a midshipman (129)
Always in luck (135)
Among the missing (153)
Building himself up (115)
Casket of diamonds, The (142)
Charades and pantomimes (188)
Cruise of the Dandy, The (141)
Every inch a boy (127)
Getting an indorser (95)
Giant islanders, The (146)
Great bonanza, The (99)
Hatchie, the guardian slave (1)
His own helper (132)
Holiday joys for bright girls and boys (150)
Honest Kit Dunstable (186)
How he won (139)
In doors and out (2)
Just his luck (105)
Little blossoms in the garden of home (154)
Living too fast (101)
Louis Chiswick's mission (182)
Lyon Hart's heroism (183)
Making a man of himself (124)
Marrying a beggar (11)
Nature's young nobleman (136)
Nature's young noblemen (136)
Nothing but a boy (104)
Oliver Optic's almanac for our boys and girls (78)
Oliver Optic's annual (117)
Oliver Optic's new story book (180)
Our little one's annual (169)
Our standard-bearer (65)
Popular amusements for school and home (189)
Prisoners of the cave, The (147)
Professor's son, The (126)
Rival battalions, The (148)

APPENDIX D
SECONDARY
BIBLIOGRAPHY

Adams, Charles Francis, Jr. "Fiction in public libraries and educational catalogues." Library Journal 4 (September-October 1879): 330-38.

Adams, Oscar Fay. A dictionary of American authors. 5th ed. rev. and enl. Boston: Houghton Mifflin Co., 1904. Reprint. Detroit: Gale Research Co., 1969.

Adams, W. Davenport. Dictionary of English literature: being a comprehensive guide to English authors and their works. 2d ed. London: Cassell Petter & Galpin, nd. Reprint. Detroit: Gale Research Co., 1966.

American book publishing record cumulative, 1876-1949: An American national bibliography. New York: R.R. Bowker Co., 1980.

American literary gazette and publishers' circular. Philadelphia: George W. Childs, 1865-1871.

Atkinson, William P. "Address." Library Journal 4 (September-October 1879): 359-62.

Austin, George L. "Lee and Shepard." The Bay State Monthly 2 (March 1885): 309-316.

"The author of one hundred successful books." The Literary Digest 14 (10 April 1897): 700.

Benet, William Rose. The reader's encyclopedia. 2d ed. New York: Crowell, 1965.

Bingham, Jane and Grace Scholt. Fifteen centuries of children's literature. An annotated chronology of British and American works in historical context. Westport, CT and London: Greenwood Press, 1980.

Blanck, Jacob. Peter Parley to Penrod. A bibliographical description of the best-loved American juvenile books.

New York: R.R. Bowker Co., 1956.

Blanck, Jacob. "A twentieth-century look at nineteenth-century children's books." In Bibliophile in the nursery edited by William Targ. Cleveland and New York: World Publishing Co., c1957. pp. 427-451.

Bragin, Charles. Dime novels bibliography 1860-1928. Brooklyn: Charles Bragin, 1938.

Bragin, Charles. Dime novels bibliography 1860-1964. Brooklyn: Charles Bragin, 1964.

British Museum general catalogue of printed books. Photolithographic edition to 1955. London: Trustees of the British Museum, 1963.

Burke, W.J. and Will D. Howe. American authors and books, 1640-1940. New York: Gramercy Publishing Co., 1943.

Carrier, Esther Jane. Fiction in public libraries, 1876-1900. New York: Scarecrow Press, 1965.

Catalogue general des livres imprimes de la bibliotheque nationale. Paris: Imprimerie Nationale, 1897.

Clarke, James Freeman. "Address." Library Journal 4 (September-October 1879): 355-57.

Commire, Anne. Something about the author. Volume 28. Detroit: Gale Research Co., 1982.

"Contributions to trade history. No. XXXVII-[XXXVIII]. Oliver Optic." American Bookseller ns 23 (1888): 289-91; ns 24 (1888): 8-11.

Cook, Michael L. Dime Novel Roundup: Annotated index 1931-1981. Bowling Green, Ohio: Bowling Green University Popular Press, 1983.

Darling, Richard. "Children's books following the Civil War." In Books in America's past: essays honoring Rudolph H. Gjelsness edited by David Kaser. Charlottesville: University Press of Virginia, 1966.

Darling, Richard L. The rise of children's book reviewing in America, 1865-1881. New York: R.R. Bowker, 1968.

Davidson, Gustav. "Little known pseudonyms of 19th century American juvenile authors." Publishers Weekly 137 (15 June 1940): 2292-95.

Davis, Dorothy R. The Carolyn Sherwin Bailey Historical Collection of children's books: a catalogue. New Haven, CT.: Southern Connecticut State College, 1967.

Dizer, John T. [untitled article on Adams]. Boys' Book Collector 1 (Fall 1969).

Dole, Nathan H., Forrest Morgan, and Caroline Ticknor. The bibliophile dictionary. New York and London: International Bibliophile Society, 1904. Reprint. Detroit: Gale Research Co., 1966.

Donelson, Kenneth and Alleen Pace Nilsen. Literature for today's young adults. Glenview, IL: Scott, Foresman, 1980.

Duyckinck, Evert A. and George L. Duyckinck. Cyclopaedia of American literature. 2 volumes. Phila.: Wm. Rutter & Co., 1875. Reprint. Detroit: Gale Research Co., 1965.

Eichelberger, Clayton L. A guide to critical reviews of United States fiction, 1870-1910. 2 volumes. Metuchen, NJ: Scarecrow Press, 1971.

Eric, Allan. "Oliver Optic." Midland Monthly 8 (December 1897): 560-62.

Field, Carolyn W. Special collections in children's literature. Chicago: American Library Association, 1982.

"For it was indeed he." Fortune 9 (April 1934): 86-90.

Fullerton, Bradford Morton. Selective bibliography of American literature 1775-1900. New York: W.F. Payson, 1932.

Gardner, Ralph D. Horatio Alger: or, The American hero era. New York: Arco Publishing Co., 1978, c1964.

Gleason, Gene. "Whatever happened to Oliver Optic?" Wilson Library Bulletin 49 (May 1975): 647-50.

Grade, Arnold E. The Merrill guide to early juvenile literature. Columbus, Ohio: C.E. Merrill, 1970.

Green, Samuel Swett. "Sensational fiction in public libraries." Library Journal 4 (September-October 1879): 345-55.

Hamilton, Sinclair. Early American book illustrators and wood engravers, 1670-1870. 2 volumes. Princeton, NJ: Princeton University Press, 1968.

Hart, James D. The Oxford Companion to American literature. 4th ed. New York: Oxford University Press, 1965.

Herzberg, Max J. The reader's encyclopedia of American literature. New York: Crowell, 1962.

Hewins, Caroline M. Books for boys and girls. Boston: Library Bureau, 1897.

Hewins, Caroline M. Books for boys and girls. 2nd ed. rev. Boston: American Library Association Publishing Board, 1904.

Hewins, Caroline M. Books for boys and girls. 3d ed. rev. Chicago: American Library Association Publishing Board, 1915.

Higginson, Thomas Wentworth. "Address." Library Journal 4 (September-October 1879): 357-59.

Hoyt, Edwin P. Horatio's boys: The life and works of Horatio Alger, Jr. Radnor, Penna.: Chilton Book Co., 1974.

Hudson, Harry K. A bibliography of hard-cover boys' books. Tampa, Fla.: Data Print, 1977.

Jameson, E.O. The biographical sketches of prominent persons, and the genealogical records of many early and other families in Medway, Mass. 1713-1886. Millis, Mass., 1886.

Johannsen, Albert. The house of Beadle and Adams and its dime and nickel novels: the story of a vanished literature. 3 volumes. Norman: University of Oklahoma Press, 1950-1962.

Johnson, Deidre. Stratemeyer pseudonyms and series books: an annotated checklist of Stratemeyer and Stratemeyer Syndicate publications. Westport, Conn.: Greenwood Press, 1982.

Jones, Dee. "William Taylor Adams: Prolific writer of boys' adventure books." Juvenile Miscellany 13 (Summer 1982): 1-7.

Jones, H.L. "The part played by Boston publishers of 1860-1900 in the field of children's books." Horn Book 45 (1969): 20-28; 153-59; 329-36.

Jones, Lynds E. The American catalogue... July 1, 1876 - December 31, 1910. New York: Peter Smith, 1941.

Jordan, Alice M. From Rollo to Tom Sawyer and other papers. Boston: Horn Book, [c1948].

Kelly, James. The American catalogue of books (original and reprints) published in the United States from Jan., 1861, to Jan., [1871]... 2 volumes. New York: Peter Smith, 1938.

Kelly, R. Gordon. Children's periodicals of the United States. Westport, Conn.: Greenwood Press, 1984.

Kilgour, Raymond L. Lee and Shepard: Publishers for the people. [s.l.]: Shoe String Press, 1965.

Kirk, John F.   A supplement to Allibone's critical dictionary of English literature and British and American
authors.   2 volumes.   Philadelphia: J.B. Lippincott & Co.,
1897.

Kunitz, Stanley J. and Howard Haycraft.   American authors
1600-1900: a biographical dictionary of American literature.
New York: H.W. Wilson Co., 1938.

Leithead, J. Edward.   "Now they're collector's items."
Boys' Book Collector 2 (1970): 154-160.

Lillibridge, Janet R.   "Chronological checklist of
books."   Dime Novel Round-up #517 (February 1976): 28-29.

Literary writings in America: a bibliography.   8 volumes.
Milwood, New York: KTO Press, 1977.

"Lothrop, Lee & Shepard Company may use the name
Lothrop."   Publishers Weekly (14 April 1906): 1172-1173.

"Lothrop, Lee & Shepard's right to the name Lothrop."
Publishers Weekly (21 April 1906): 1219.

Lyons, Betty L.   "A history of children's magazines
published in the United States from 1789-1899."   (Ph.D.
dissertation, Johns Hopkins University, 1942.)

Macpherson, J.A.   "Oliver Optic."   National Magazine
(Boston) 7: 58.

Mahoney, Bertha E.   Illustrator's of children's books.
Boston: The Horn Book, 1947.

Maxwell, Barbara.   Checklist of children's books, 1837-
1876.   Philadelphia: Free Library of Philadelphia, 1975.

Mott, Frank L.   A history of American magazines.   5
volumes.   Cambridge: Harvard University Press, 1938-1968.

Munsey, Frank A.   "Two veteran authors."   Munsey's
Magazine 8 (October 1892): 58-61.

Munsey, Frank A.   "William Taylor Adams."   Munsey's
Magazine (October 1886).

National cyclopaedia of American biography.   New York:
J.T. White & Co., 1898.

The National Union catalog: Pre-1956 imprints.   London:
Mansell, 1968.

The National Union catalog: Pre-1956 imprints. Supplement.   London: Mansell, 1980.

[Obituary of W.T. Adams].   Book News (Philadelphia) 15
(1897): 465.

[Obituary of W.T. Adams]. Golden Days 18 (1 May 1897): 376.

[Obituary of W.T. Adams]. New York Evening Post (27 March 1897).

[Obituary of W.T. Adams]. New York Press (28 March 1897).

[Obituary of W.T. Adams]. Publishers Weekly 51 (1897): 629.

"Oliver Optic." Critic 30 (3 April 1897): 242-43.

"Oliver Optic and his school." Literary News 18 (April 1897): 116.

"Oliver Optic passes away." New York Herald (28 March 1897): section 3, p. 4.

"Oliver Optic's method." Bookman 30 (November 1909): 223.

Pickering, Sam. "A boy's own war." New England Quarterly 48 (September 1975): 362-377.

Prager, Arthur. Rascals at large; or, The clue in the old nostalgia. Garden City, New York: Doubleday, 1971.

Publishers weekly, the book industry journal. New York: Bowker, 1872-   .

Pullar, Elizabeth. "Oliver Optic - The prince of story tellers." Spinning Wheel 35 (October 1979): 20-23.

Richards, Robert Fulton. Concise dictionary of American literature. New York: Philosophical Library, Inc., 1955. Reprint. New York: Greenwood Press, 1969.

Roorbach, Orville A. Supplement to the Bibliotheca Americana: a catalogue of American publications from October, 1852, to May, 1855... New York: Peter Smith, 1939.

Sabin, Joseph. Bibliotheca Americana. A dictionary of books relating to America, from its discovery to the present time. New York: Sabin, 1868-1892; Bibliographical Society of America, 1928-1936.

Sarkissian, Adele. Children's authors and illustrators: an index to biographical dictionaries. 3rd ed. Detroit: Gale Research Co., 1981.

Shaw, John Mackay. Childhood in poetry. Detroit: Gale Research Co., 1967.

Shaw, John Mackay. Childhood in poetry. Supplement. Detroit: Gale Research Co., 1972.

Shaw, John Mackay. Childhood in poetry. Supplement 2.
Detroit: Gale Research Co., 1976.

Shaw, John Mackay. Childhood in poetry. Supplement 3.
Detroit: Gale Research Co., 1980.

Smith, Elva S. The history of children's literature: A
syllabus with selected bibliographies. rev. and enl. ed. by
Margaret Hodges and Susan Steinfirst. Chicago: American
Library Association, 1980.

Steinhauer, Donald L. Golden Days [index]. Dime Novel
Round-up bibliographic listing. Supplement no. 1, 1957(?).

Stern, Madeleine B. Publishers for mass entertainment
in nineteenth century America. Boston: G.K. Hall, 1980.

Stevens, William O. "William Taylor Adams." Dictionary
of American biography. v.I, p.102-03. New York: Charles
Scribner's Sons, 1928.

Tanselle, G. Thomas. Guide to the study of United States
imprints. 2 volumes. Cambridge, MA: The Belknap Press of
Harvard University Press, 1971.

Tebbel, John. From rags to riches: Horatio Alger, Jr.,
and the American dream. New York: Macmillan, 1963.

Tebbel, John. A history of book publishing in the United
States. 3 volumes. New York: R.R. Bowker, 1975-1978.

The United States Catalogue Supplement [1902-1905].
Minneapolis: H. W. Wilson Co., 1906.

The United States Catalogue 1912. Minneapolis & New
York: H.W. Wilson Company, 1912.

The United States Catalogue 1928. New York: H.W. Wilson
Company, 1928.

University of Florida Libraries. Index to the Baldwin
Library of books in English before 1900, primarily for children. 3 volumes. Boston: G.K. Hall & Co., 1981.

Van Devier, Roy B. "Oliver Optic." Boys' Book Collector
3 (1971): 215-18.

Van Doren, Charles. Webster's American biographies.
Springfield, Mass.: G.&C. Merriam Co., 1974.

Wallace, William Stewart. Dictionary of North American
authors deceased before 1950. Toronto: Ryerson Press, 1951.
Reprint. Detroit: Gale Research Co., 1968.

Wallen, S.E. "Oliver Optic (William Taylor Adams) as
author and editor (Pt.1)." Dime Novel Round-up #511 (April
1975): 26-35.

Wallen, S.E.   "Oliver Optic (William Taylor Adams) as author and editor (Pt. 2)." Dime Novel Round-up #512 (May 1975): 38-46.

Walther, Peter C.   "William Taylor Adams: a literary retrospection." Dime Novel Round-up #548 (April 1981): 26-36.

Warner, Charles Dudley. Biographical dictionary and synopsis of books ancient and modern. Akron, Ohio: Werner Co., 1902. Reprint. Detroit: Gale Research Co., 1965.

Wilson, James G. and John Fiske. Appletons' cyclopaedia of American biography. New York: D. Appleton and Co., 1887.

Wright, Lyle H. American fiction: 1851-1875. A contribution toward a bibliography. San Marino, CA: The Huntington Library, 1957.

Wright, Lyle H. American fiction: 1876-1900. A contribution toward a bibliography. San Marino, CA: The Huntington Library, 1972.

ILLUSTRATORS AND ENGRAVERS

Included are those illustrators and engravers whose work appears in William Taylor Adams's books, edited magazines, and serializations. The number in parenthesis refers to the CHRONOLOGICAL LIST entry number.

ANDREW, GEORGE T.
(engraver)

Our little ones and the
  nursery (118)
Story and song. For all
  winter long (151)

ANDREW, JOHN
1815-1875 (engraver)

All aboard (4)
Birthday party, The (23)
Boat club, The (3)
Careless Kate (25)
Christmas gift, The (20)
Coming wave, The (91)
Cringle and cross-tree (79)
Cross and crescent (85)
Do-somethings, The (29)
Dolly and I (21)
Dorcas Club, The (92)
Down the Rhine (72)
Gold thimble, The (28)
Great bonanza, The (99)
Isles of the sea (106)
Little Bobtail (84)
Little by little (15)
Little merchant, The (18)
Money-maker (89)
Now or never (5)
Ocean-born (96)

ANDREW, JOHN (continued)
Out west (103)
Palace and cottage (67)
Picnic party, The (27)
Poor and proud (9)
Proud and lazy (24)
Robinson Crusoe, Jr. (26)
Sea and shore (82)
Soldier boy, The (36)
Sunny shores (93)
Try again (6)
Uncle Ben (22)
Up the Baltic (80)
Yacht club, The (87)
Young lieutenant, The (42)
Young voyagers, The (19)

BARRY, CHARLES A.
1830-1892 (illustrator)

Yankee middy, The (44)

BILLINGS, HAMMATT
1818-1874 (illustrator)

All aboard (4)
Birthday party, The (23)
Boat club, The (3)
Careless Kate (25)
Christmas gift, The (20)
Do-somethings, The (29)

INDEX 2
MAGAZINES, SERIES, AND SHORT-TITLES

References are to entry numbers, not page numbers. Series
titles are in capitals; magazine titles are underlined.
A number without a qualifier refers to the CHRONOLOGICAL
LIST. Reference to other sections are preceded by the
abbreviations listed below:

> AS = Author Series   P = Publisher
> PS = Publisher's Series S = Serialization

About the Compiler

DOLORES BLYTHE JONES is Assistant Curator of the de Grummond Collection at the University of Southern Mississippi. Her earlier works include *Children's Literature Awards and Winners.*

www.ingramcontent.com/pod-product-compliance
Lightning Source LLC
Chambersburg PA
CBHW070445100426
42812CB00004B/1211